Chicago's

Unsolved Crimes & Mysteries

Bryan W. Alaspa

Schiffer Publishing Ltd®

4880 Lower Valley Road • Atglen, PA 19310

Dedication

For my brother, Marc,
the best brother anyone could ever possibly ask for.

Schiffer Books" are available at special discounts for bulk purchases for sales promotions or premiums. Special editions, including personalized covers, corporate imprints, and excerpts can be created in large quantities for special needs. For more information contact the publisher.

Published by Schiffer Publishing, Ltd.
4880 Lower Valley Road
Atglen, PA 19310
Phone: (610) 593-1777; Fax: (610) 593-2002
E-mail: Info@schifferbooks.com

For the largest selection of fine reference books on this and related subjects,
please visit our website at **www.schifferbooks.com.**
You may also write for a free catalog.

This book may be purchased from the publisher.
Please try your bookstore first.

We are always looking for people to write books on new and related subjects.
If you have an idea for a book, please contact us at
proposals@schifferbooks.com.

In Europe, Schiffer books are distributed by
Bushwood Books
6 Marksbury Ave.
Kew Gardens
Surrey TW9 4JF England
Phone: 44 (0) 20 8392 8585; Fax: 44 (0) 20 8392 9876
E-mail: info@bushwoodbooks.co.uk
Website: www.bushwoodbooks.co.uk

text by Bryan W. Alaspa

Other Schiffer Books by the Author:

Ghosts of St. Louis: The Lemp Mansion and Other Eerie Tales
ISBN: 978-0-7643-2688-2 $12.95

Chicago Crime Stories: Rich Gone Wrong
ISBN: 978-0-7643-3114-5 $14.99

Chicago Disasters
ISBN: 978-0-7643-3395-8 $14.99

Designed by Mark David Bowyer
Type set in ITC Avant Garde Gothic Demi / Book Antiqua

ISBN: 978-0-7643-4311-7
Printed in The United States of America

Contents

Acknowledgments

I would like to take a moment to thank one of the most amazing women I have ever known, Melanie Parker. She is the love of my life and now is my wife. Hopefully, by the time this book hits the shelves, she will actually *be* my wife. She is the best person to bounce ideas off. She is also one of the biggest encouragers and one of the harshest editors. If you come to a book reading or book signing and see the beautiful blonde woman sitting there nearby, that's her. I would also like to thank my mom and dad and my family for their love and encouragement over the years. I love you all and thank you for your support. A thank you also goes to John Spira's sister, Stephanie Spira McNeil. She provided me with key information on the John Spira case.

Introduction
A Mysterious City

Any city with a history as long and colorful as Chicago's is bound to have just a few mysteries. This is true of a place that, for all intents and purposes, was founded on blood. Before it was a city, it was a fort known as Fort Dearborn. Not long after the fort was established, and people began to come there for shelter and to start their lives in what was, then, a wilderness, war broke out between settlers, the French, and Native Americans. Hundreds were slaughtered at Fort Dearborn when the Native Americans played a ruse that looked like they were going to let the settlers and soldiers go, but decided to slaughter them instead. Thus, the very ground that Chicago would be built upon was baptized in blood.

However, like many places, with so many people gathered in one place, there are mysteries in and around Chicago that just cannot be explained through conventional means. Some of these unexplained phenomena have passed into the realm of urban legend. With those, many of the stories can be dismissed. Since so many Chicago residents are from so many different cultures, their effect on the mysteries cannot be dismissed. Each culture has its own beliefs in ghosts, angels, demons, and the like, and some of the supposed "mysteries," when filtered through those lenses, can be explained with a more critical eye.

Chicago is a city that has suffered through disaster after disaster. It is a working-class city and its attitudes towards disasters and mysteries is a working-class one. People in Chicago know that the city has a rich history of violence and mayhem, but they also know that the people will come together when disaster strikes and build up a city that is stronger and more united than it was before the disaster hit. The same, in some ways, can be said about the strange, the bizarre, and the unsolved. They become stories. They become legends. They become part of the fabric of the city and its history and, at times, there is a strange Chicago pride about these legends, mysteries, and bizarre tales.

Still, there are so many stories and so many neighborhoods and people in Chicago that not everything can be explained away by science or skepticism. While not every story in this book has some kind of supernatural bent to it, some of them defy explanation at this time. Some may be fueled by imagination, and over-active ones at that. However, some surely have a human reason behind them, and a potentially sinister human motive to boot.

Yes, Chicago is notorious for its criminal history. The sheer number of unsolved mysteries involving disappeared people and unsolved murders in Chicago is staggering. How many gangsters offed one of their competition and then disposed of the body so well that they were never seen again? The estimates must be astronomical. However, few, if any, of those have become famous. This book tries to deal with some of the more famous ones.

There is the possibility that each of these mysteries has a reasonable explanation. Perhaps, in time, they will be solved. In the meantime, however, these are the mysteries that still baffle Chicagoans. These are the stories that are discussed in hushed tones in homes across the region or argued over loudly in bars as drunken experts put forth theories and claim to have all of the answers.

Some of the mysteries in this book definitely qualify as supernatural. Some of them are so strange that many still refuse to believe them. However, all of them were reported, have been discussed, and, most of them, reported in the newspapers and local media.

Chicago has always been a strange place. These stories could prove that it may be a place even stranger than we realize. So, take a journey into the bizarre and strange in one of the biggest and most beautiful — but complicated — cities on the planet.

Part One
UFOs and the Supernatural

Every city has them. Every city with even a modest history has its share of ghost stories. Some ghosts are actually synonymous with certain locations. Chicago is no different. There are certain ghosts and tales that find their home in the Windy City.

Like most cities, there are also tales of *things*: visitors that come from other planets. Of course, in Chicago, sometimes these tales are told as if a joke. As long as the working day can continue uninterrupted, whether or not aliens might have visited some part of town is irrelevant. And, anyway, why wouldn't some intergalactic tourist not want to visit Wrigley Field or catch a Cubs game.

In some areas, the tales of ghosts and the supernatural are interwoven within the fabric of the culture and neighborhood that surrounds it. In some cases, the ghosts inhabit places that have been around since the city first formed. In other cases, the ghosts seem sad and haunt places that modern Chicago residents have long forgotten.

There may be logical explanations for any and all of the tales within this chapter. A practical person would point to overactive imaginations, tall-tales told repeatedly until believed, and even weather phenomenon for likely explanations. Most Chicagoans probably, in their hearts, know that those are the real explanations. Still, at night, when tales of the strange are told, these accounts can seem all too real. Some of them are not even that old. And every year, the tales become more detailed, more exaggerated, and more elements are added.

These are the ghosts and otherworldy visitors to Chicago.

Chapter One
Otherworldly Visitors to Chicago's Busiest Airport

Chicago has always been a transportation hub. There was a time when nearly all roads heading west, headed through Chicago. Siting the Great Lake of Lake Michigan, it was also a major port where goods were transported from the exterior of the country to the interior and vice versa. Then, when trains became the prominent mode of transportation, the great railroads of the time made Chicago their hub. Its location near the middle of the country made it the perfect place for roads, railroads, and more to go right through before dispersing to the rest of the country.

There was even a time when the city was intended to become a major hub when it came to airship transportation. Buildings across the city and any open fields located in or around it were going to become places where passengers would board and de-board from luxurious airships. However, an accident that sent an airship into a Chicago skyscraper, killing almost all of those on board the ship and many more inside the building, put an end to that.

Even though the idea of turning Chicago into a "blimpopolis" went down in flames that day, the idea of turning the city into a major air transportation hub did not. Eventually, an airfield on the south side of the city, now known as Midway Airport, became one of the busiest airports on the planet during the days when passenger planes were relatively small and used propellers to move them through the air. When the world began moving towards jet planes as the predominant mode of transportation, it was obvious that Midway was much too small and its runways too short. Another solution was sought.

On the north side of town was a space that originally had been developed for a testing facility for Douglas C-54 aircraft during World War II. When Midway airport began to become obsolete, the city developers and aviation experts looked at what was then known as Orchard Field Airport. They thought that they would have the necessary space to keep the site growing and developing as the needs of airplanes advanced over the years. They began to develop the airport into the major hub that it eventually became.

For years, O'Hare Airport was the busiest in the world. In recent years, that title has gone to some other airports around the world. However, on certain days and at certain times of the year, such as during holidays, the airport on the north side of Chicago becomes the busiest airport in the world again. Thousands of planes take off and land at O'Hare, and these are large jets. The planes range from private Lear jets to super-sized 747s, and they come from all over the world, bringing thousands upon thousands of passengers into and through Chicago on a daily basis. It is also a major hub for major airlines such as United and American.

The radar facilities that manage the traffic in and around Chicago are some of the most powerful in the world. Their range is huge and affects much of the air traffic across the entire United States. When there are radar problems at O'Hare Airport, it cascades across the country and affects hundreds and thousands of flights taking off and landing at other airports. While other airports, such as those in Atlanta and Moscow, may have become busier on a more consistent basis, there is no denying that Chicago's O'Hare International Airport is a major powerhouse for air traffic in the U. S. Thousands upon thousands of travelers rely on operations at the airport and among the air traffic controllers to run smoothly, so that they can get to their destinations safely. Given the sheer numbers of airplanes and passengers that are in, out, and through O'Hare each and every day, the airport has an amazing safety record with only one major air disaster in its entire history.

This is why it is very disturbing when things suddenly appear over the airfield, potentially affecting hundreds of flights. It is especially disturbing when this particular anomaly is not seen on radar or by anyone in the air traffic control tower. Such a thing would have to be impossible, surely.

A Visitor to O'Hare

However, on November 7, 2006, at about 4:15 in the afternoon, a visitor from somewhere other than the planet Earth may have visited O'Hare International Airport.

It was a typical November day in the Chicago area. Often the temperatures in the Windy City turn towards the cold and snowy as soon as August departs. When that happens, the city often spends months covered in gray clouds, awaiting the snow and the blustery winds. It was cloudy that day, just like many others to come.

That did not stop or slow down anything going on in and around O'Hare Airport, however. The radar waves of the control tower easily penetrated the low-hanging cloud cover. The base of the clouds hovered just above the airport, at about 1,900 feet. For O'Hare, clouds are nothing to get worried about and there was no rain or snow in the forecast. Thousands of goods and people were being transported in and out of the airport, just like always, that particular afternoon. There was not a single fluctuation in the airport's power, its services, or its operations at any point during the course of that day. There was nothing that would indicate that this particular November 7 was going to be different from any other.

Gate C-17 exists near what investigators would call the "geometric center" of the entire airport. Air traffic did not go directly over this part of the airport, but the runways and air traffic did continue on, unrelenting, all around. This was the part of the terminal used by United Airlines, one of the biggest and busiest airlines in the world. O'Hare Airport is United's international hub and the location of the company's headquarters. That November 7, for United Airlines, everything was routine and proceeding as normal, albeit busy, as always. This was even true at gate C-17 which had already seen a number of airplanes come, pick up passengers, then pull away, and take off again.

At gate C-17 a ramp mechanic was getting set to push back a Boeing 737-500 from the gate. He was standing near the nose of the plane, in communication with other mechanics, as well as the tower and the pilots sitting above him in the cockpit. He was wearing a headset to communicate with the others and the cord was plugged into an outlet beneath the nose of the plane. This would help provide easy communication between himself and the pilots. The night was cold and growing dark even by that time, the hours having just changed now that Halloween had passed, bringing darkness to the city much faster than just a month earlier.

Probably tired and just wishing that the tower would give clearance so that the plane could be pushed away, this ramp mechanic would later tell investigators that he had a sudden and overpowering compulsion to look over his head. What he saw there would send shivers down his spine that had nothing to do with the cold Chicago wind and everything to do with something hovering squarely over gate C-17.

The mechanic said he saw a disc, definitely metallic, rotating in place above the gate. It made no sound and emitted no light. If the strange object was making any noise, it could not be heard by the mechanic over the roar of nearby jet engines or the headset he wore. When he looked up, he would tell investigators, it was about 4:30 p.m.

He thought that it was strange. He did not panic. Instead, he calmly used his headset to call the operation control center. This is not the air traffic control tower, but the people who control the traffic in and around the gates and ramps. The woman who was in charge of that section of the gate area was named Sue. He reported that there was something, and something darn strange, hovering over his gate. Sue was responsible for ten gates that day and probably thought that this mechanic was having a joke at her expense. Given how busy O'Hare is, that kind of nonsense was the kind of thing that could get a ramp mechanic fired. She noted the incident and then asked if he was kidding and when he said no, she made note of that as well. Standard procedure meant that she had to file the notification and she needed to alert the tower to the possibility that something was hovering over a gate, with the chance that it could stray right into busy air space.

The ramp mechanic then realized that he was probably being overheard by the pilots in the cockpit above him. Did they see what he was seeing? He called up to them and asked if they wouldn't mind leaning out their windows and looking up and determining if he was really seeing what he was seeing or, perhaps, in need of a very long holiday vacation.

Pilot and co-pilot, according to the mechanic, opened the small windows of the cockpit, sure that this was all some kind of elaborate joke. Instead, both of them expressed shock to the ramp mechanic that there was, indeed, some kind of gray metal, circular object hovering over the gate.

When investigators came and began asking questions, months later, after the story had broken in the Chicago news, the ramp mechanic would swear that he was not alone in seeing this object. In fact, his best guess was that dozens of people had seen it. He guessed that the object was anywhere from 500 to 1,000 feet in the air. He watched it for what he estimated to be two minutes before, suddenly, without warning, the object shot up into the sky at near-blinding speed, punching its way through the clouds. It punched its way through the clouds so hard and so fast that it left a perfect circular hole in the clouds that showed clear blue skies above it. This hole was perfectly round and stayed there for several minutes before more clouds moved in and covered it.

That should have been it. One ramp mechanic and some pilots saw something a bit weird and then it was gone, end of story, right? Not really.

11

Other witnesses soon came forward. As outside resources began to investigate the incident, they managed to talk to one of the pilots in the plane that was sitting outside gate C-17. He confirmed that he and his pilot were in the cockpit and overheard the ground technician talking about the strange object. He and the pilot opened the small windows in their cockpit and looked up and he confirmed that a disc-shaped object hovered above the gate. This pilot was in the left cockpit seat at the time and he confirmed that neither him nor the other pilot had a camera with which to take a photo of the object. Both of the cockpit crew members laughed, making jokes about what they thought was something that could easily be explained.

Just across the way were two more mechanics. They were inside the cockpit of another United Airlines plane that was to be taxied to a garage for maintenance. There were two people inside the cockpit there, one in each seat. When the first broadcasts came over their radio, they too laughed. Then the radio, according to their reports, suddenly burst into life with chatter from all around the airport about the strange object hovering over the gate. The mechanic in the left pilot seat began to taxi the airplane across the field, heading to a large maintenance hangar where the plane would be serviced.

The two mechanics continued to hear the nervous chatter over their radio. No one seemed to want to take the sighting seriously. As they began to taxi, the mechanic in the driver's seat looked out his window. At the angle in which they were taxiing the plane, he had a perfect view of gate C-17 out his left window. He looked up and was astonished to see that there was an object hovering over the gate. He said it was metallic, gray in color, and hovering in place. He guessed that it was maybe 200 feet beneath the base of the clouds. It did not emit any light and it did not appear to be rotating from where he was sitting.

Hoping to prove that he was not crazy, he asked his seat-mate if he could see the object. Since his seat-mate was on the other side of the cockpit, he could not easily lean out the window closest to him and see the object. He also could not see the object when he leaned down to look up and out the window, since the object was just too high for him to see. However, once the plane rounded a corner and put the object on the opposite side of the cockpit, his seat-mate said that he could see it. He said he saw it just in time to rocket off through the clouds, leaving that strange perfectly round hole in the clouds. When the plane reached its destination, the mechanic in the left seat looked back and saw that hole in the clouds.

Both men were shaken. They could not believe what they had just seen. Just as they were getting out of the cockpit, the tower radioed to an incoming plane, a Gateway Airlines plane, to look and see if they saw a disc-shaped object hovering over the airport. The pilots on that plane laughed and the air traffic controller did, as well. By that point, the object had already shot up through the clouds and the pilots stated that they did not see anything. At that time, the mechanics who had taxied the plane to the hangar broke in on the transmission and said that they had seen the object. They did not identify themselves by name, but said they were mechanics and they had been moving a plane to a maintenance hangar.

Another employee of the airport was sitting at his desk, buried in paperwork and wishing that the day would just hurry up. He had a radio on his desk, listening to the every-day chatter from the mechanics and the tower. The air around the airport was always alive with radio chatter from the gates to the runways to the planes and the tower. O'Hare Airport is also so big that it has its own police and fire department. At any time the radio chatter in the airport was deafening. One thing soon cut across that chatter to this employee.

He stood up, looking for a chance to see what they were talking about. He did not, at that time, think that it was a UFO. One person on the radio said that they thought it might have been some kind of weather balloon. While that was a logical explanation, it was also a problem if a weather balloon had gotten off track and was now drifting into the busiest air space in the country. If it was some other kind of balloon, one big enough to be seen all around the airport, this was another problem. It was especially worrisome if the tower could not see the object on radar or visually.

When he reached a nearby gate, he walked out into the noisy tarmac area. He looked up and let his jaw drop. Indeed, there was the object. He would say later that he had a little trouble locating the gray object against the gray background of the clouds, but he knew where to look. It hovered there, silently, for minutes. He would tell investigators that it was not a balloon and not any kind of aircraft he had ever seen before. He also said that no one, in his estimation, who worked for the airport or airlines would risk the legal implications or their career by making a joke or pulling some kind of prank. He said the object appeared fuzzy at the ends and beneath, but was clear and easily defined at the top. Then, to his amazement, the object shot through the clouds, vanishing through the hole it made, moving at a slight angle.

This employee would tell investigators that he was astonished by what he saw. He did not file an immediate report, but talked to investigators later and said, had he seen anything like this again, he would likely file some kind of report.

Pilots and crew around the airport reportedly saw the object. At first, the airline, the airport, and the FAA thought nothing of it. It was noted in the tower logs, but the recordings of air traffic controllers seem to show a lack of concern over the object. In fact, they seem to be joking about the supposed sighting, which seemed strange to many since any object, even if you believed that it was not extraterrestrial in origin, hovering over the airport constituted a possible hazard.

Pilots reportedly refused to file reports that they had seen anything. It was still considered professional suicide to make a UFO report filing. Reportedly, a passenger on another plane, having a chat with a pilot, stated that this pilot said that no one who wanted to continue flying would file such a report. It was the surest way to end up in a psychiatric evaluation and then sitting behind a desk for the rest of your career.

The FAA, United Airlines, and O'Hare Airport denied that anything had happened, at least at first. However, the people who had seen the object were having their own crises in dealing with it. They faced ridicule from their co-workers, but at least one of them was having deep religious issues reconciling what he had seen with what he believed was true about the universe. It was a reporter for the *Chicago Tribune*, hearing about the issue and filing a Freedom of Information Act claim that finally broke the story.

In January of 2008, the story was finally printed in the *Chicago Tribune*. Prior to that time, *Chicago Tribune* writer John Hilkevitch was just the newspaper's transportation reporter. He had a job that, in a city like Chicago, was necessary, but hardly the kind of thing that garnered him a lot of attention. When those who had seen the UFO were willing to talk to him and he began writing a series of stories about the incident, he suddenly found himself on a global stage. News agencies from around the globe wanted to know what had happened at one of the world's busiest airports.

Footage leaked of Hilkevitch having an off-camera conversation with a news anchor on the local Chicago 24-hour news channel known as CLTV. In that conversation Hilkevitch says he has been getting phone calls from people all over the world, including some very prominent professors and people who claim to be experts in the world of UFOs. He also says that the FAA has continued to deny that there was any incident and even implies that there is a cover up afoot.

As for the incident itself, it eventually passed into history. The FAA came out and said that they felt the incident was caused by weather phenomenon. They blamed the low cloud cover mixed with lights from the airport as the cause. What caused the perfectly round hole in the clouds that let blue sky shine through? The FAA has no explanation for that.

Some experts believe that to create such a hole, the object would had to have been moving at incredible speeds and emitting some kind of energy. They theorize that the object literally burned its way through the cloud level and into the clear air above. They also believe that only an object that was perfectly round and disc-shaped could have done it.

The people who saw the object that day continue to stick by their story. Every year, around the time that the incident happened, John Hilkevitch finds himself as the *Chicago Tribune's* UFO expert and does interviews. The FAA and the officials at O'Hare have nothing further to say on the issue. As far as the FAA is concerned, it was a weather incident and they have no plans to investigate the situation further.

The employees who saw the object, however, say that they know what they saw and what they saw made them question everything they know about the known universe. For some, the sighting of that strange circular object on that November day was a major event in their lives, when their entire opinion about the universe was turned on its head.

What was the object? To this day, no one knows. Life, such as it is, has returned to normal at O'Hare International Airport. But, perhaps, for just a moment on one day in November of 2007, O'Hare International Airport was not just one of the busiest airports on planet Earth, but one of the busiest airports in the entire galaxy.

Chapter Two
Chicago's Famous Ghosts

Since Chicago is as big and old as it is, it has more than its share of ghost stories. There are roads in and around Chicago that are supposedly haunted. There are places where famous murders have taken place that are rumored to still be haunted. There are buildings that are now condominiums and homes that are considered haunted. There are even bars and restaurants that many claim are filled with haunts and spirits that just will not rest.

However, there are a few haunted locations that are more famous than others. Some of them are famous just within the Chicago area, talked about in hushed tones by residents or teenagers daring each other to visit these locations. A couple, though, have become so famous among ghost hunters that, on any given night, you would likely to see more ghost hunting parties than actual ghosts in some instances.

These are the famous ghosts of Chicago. Even if you do not believe in ghosts, you'll have to admit that some of these stories are fantastic and just outright strange.

Bachelor's Grove Cemetery

One of the most haunted places on the entire planet is supposedly located on the south side of the city of Chicago. Technically speaking, the cemetery of Bachelor's Grove is not within the city limits of Chicago, but near the southern suburb of Midlothian. However, its fame among those looking to make contact with the spirits is legendary and reaches all the way around the world. So famous is Bachelor's Grove as a haunt hunter's paradise that the police and residents who still live anywhere in and around the cemetery have tried their best to make it impossible to find. But ghost hunters still find ways to get to the small plot.

When you find your way into Bachelor's Grove, there really isn't much to look at. The cemetery headstones are in disrepair and many of them have been the target of vandalism. The entire cemetery is overgrown with weeds and vegetation. The cemetery proper is ringed with a chain-link fence and there is a heavy, locked gate that is supposed to bar anyone from coming in and disturbing the graves and their headstones. Of course, this does not stop intrepid ghost hunters with limitless gall and wire cutters.

There hasn't been anyone buried in Bachelor's Grove Cemetery for a long time now. However, there was a time when the area was more like a park and a cemetery mixed into one. There was a time when an active and bustling community sprouted up around the cemetery. Bachelor's Grove was first designated as a place for the dead way back in 1844.

Many believe that it was first settled by "Yankee Farmers" who had settled into the area. This claim was made by a former caretaker for the cemetery for a newspaper article published in the late '70s. However, there are gravestones in the cemetery that go back well before that. What is known is that maps from those days show the cemetery and a town around the burial area. At one time, that town was on a major thoroughfare through the area known as the Midlothian Turnpike. When the highway system was built in the 1950s, it bypassed the turnpike and it became a much smaller and more seldom-traveled road. When that happened, the residents who lived in and around Bachelor's Grove Cemetery eventually up and left.

At one time, it is believed that the cemetery was quite peaceful and beautiful. It is situated right on a very deep pond that must have looked quite lovely during certain times of year. The grass was well kept back then. Given the nationalities of the communities around the cemetery at the time, it was likely families would spend Sundays picnicking in the cemetery, eating with their deceased relatives, in a manner of speaking.

For a time, the road leading to Bachelor's Grove was easy to find, just off of the Midlothian Turnpike. However, curiosity-seekers and ghost hunters were creating too much of a problem for those who still had to drive that road, and most of the people who visited the site were not nearly as respectful of the gravesites as they should have been. When the residents left, the cemetery fell into disrepair. The road that led to the cemetery became overgrown and harder to find. Also, there were rumors that Satanists and other cults and mischief makers were using the cemetery for nefarious purposes. There were even rumors that during the height of Chicago's famous gangster era, mobsters were using the deep lake beside the cemetery to dispose of bodies.

When rumors about how haunted the cemetery was began to grow, people in the area, including the Illinois State Police and the Forrest Preserve officials, who now run the property, did all they could to further hide the access to the little cemetery. However, the road it still there, looking like little more than a dirt trail leading into the woods. The cemetery itself is sad, in its way, forgotten and left to slowly rot and fall apart, helped along by vandals and people with little to no respect for the dead.

Though police have since done everything they could to make it harder to get to the actual cemetery, it hasn't deterred curosity seekers and ghost hunters. Intrepid ghost hunters have to park and spend time searching for the entrance road. Now, stiff penalties and fines can be levied against anyone who is found on the road or in the cemetery, and patrols of police cars are stepped up around certain times of the year, such as Halloween. There is a chain across the road, should anyone attempt to take a four-wheel drive vehicle down its path, and a fence with a gate has been erected over the entrance to the cemetery proper.

However, the fame of the cemetery, if anything, has only grown. Over the years, people have come from around the country in hopes of seeing some of the strange things that are reported to occur within the creepy chain-linked barriers of Bachelor's Grove. You see, Bachelor's Grove has some truly bizarre reports of ghosts, and many of them are unlike anything ghost hunters find anywhere else.

For example, there is a report that along the path to the cemetery, some have come across a phantom house. Yes, a house itself that may be a ghost. Those who have seen it say that they find the house while walking down the creepy, overgrown path leading to the cemetery. All around them are the woods, nature, and vegetation that has grown over the road. Many say it is noticeably colder when walking down the path than it is when you are trying to find it from the road.

A Phantom House

Somewhere along the way, the sound of squeaking, like that of a porch swing chain, can be heard. Many have come across a beautiful white house complete with porch and supposed swing in the middle of the woods. There is a white picket fence around the property as well and many a surprised ghost hunter has attempted to enter this mysterious home. However, they usually find that the image recedes as they try to get closer, until it slowly fades away into the night or the dimming light.

Many say that this was the former house of the cemetery caretaker. Explorers have found evidence that a house used to exist on the property. There is little left anymore except for a few stones and some indication of a foundation. Even the houses that once resided in Bachelor's Grove cannot leave.

Phantom Cars

There have also been reports of phantom cars. Most of these come from the road and path that leads from the Midlothian Turnpike to the cemetery. Usually, the car is seen moving in the opposite direction from those heading for the cemetery. The car is described most often as very old and out of date. Cars are sometimes seen sitting by the side of the road right on the Turnpike, as well, and then vanish whenever anyone tries to approach.

Hauntings

Inside the cemetery, ghost hunters have said they have run across a number of typical haunting anomalies. However, few ghost hunters, in other areas that are rumored to be haunted, have come across a ghostly farmer and his spirit horse that seem to patrol the fence area of Bachelor's Grove.

The story is that a farmer once used the land near the cemetery. One day, while the farmer was out tending to his field, the horse he was using to pull the plow suddenly went crazy. The two of them ran towards the deep lake that sits to one side of the cemetery. Both of them went in and both of them drowned. Rumor has it that the man and his horse can still be seen from time to time, plowing their fields and exchanging strange glances with the people of today.

Then there is the reported two-headed ghost that also is rumored to run amidst the headstones of Bachelor's Grove. No one knows for sure how this ghost came to be, or who he might be, or why he has two heads. However, there are many visitors who claim that they have seen him.

Once, in the 1970s, a group of ghost hunters found the road and made the trek down the path to the cemetery. They began to take photographs of the headstones and the trees. When they got back to their lab and processed the film, one of the photographers saw what clearly seemed to be a woman in white sitting on one of the headstones. She appears to be sitting there casually, her legs crossed and her head facing away from the picture-taker. The photographer insists that no one was there when it was taken.

As for the rest, most ghost hunters claim that their photos are filled with orbs, or balls of white light that they say are the manifestation of spirits on this particular plane of existence. Their photos are filled with white and blue orbs, as well as white mists and mysterious shapes that they insist mean they have absolute proof that Bachelor's Grove is haunted.

These same ghost hunters also have numerous recordings called EVPs, or Electronic Voice Phenomenon. Most ghost hunters carry tape recorders or digital recorders with them. They then ask questions of the spirits and, although they cannot hear the responses at the time when asking the questions, they clearly hear them when they listen back later. Ghost hunters at Bachelor's Grove have heard male and female voices, plus the sounds of animals, such as horses and even wolves. Of course, there are no wolves in Illinois, but the recordings certainly do sound like them if you listen closely enough.

Disrepair and Dangerous

As for the cemetery, it continues to slowly fall into disrepair. There have been those who have wanted to fix it up, and there have been people who have repaired the headstones and attempted to clear away the weeds and overgrowth. However, some people seeking ghosts and proof of the afterlife continue to visit the cemetery and create damage. These days, most people who now live in the area just hope the cemetery vanishes and people stop trying to visit.

However, the fame of Bachelor's Grove grows instead of shrinks. The busiest time seems to be around Halloween and many teenagers still flock to the area to try to test each other's nerve and see who can spend the most time in the cemetery without being afraid. The police, however, say that the state of disrepair for the path leading to the cemetery, plus all of the overgrown roots and fallen trees and headstones, makes exploring Bachelor's Grove Cemetery too dangerous. They warn those who come from miles around in hopes of seeing the phantom house, the phantom cars, the White Lady, or any of the other famous ghosts and haunts, that they take the trespassing on that property very seriously. Stiff fines and arrests can be made against anyone caught by the police on the grounds of Bachelor's Grove.

Resurrection Mary

Imagine driving down a dark road. It is late at night and you are barely able to pay attention to the white lines that delineate the road in front of you. Suddenly, out of the gloom, you see a young woman standing beside the road. She looks lost and out of place standing there, and she looks scared. Her thumb is out and she's evidently looking for a ride. It is far too late for a girl that young to be out and it is especially bad that she seems to be hitchhiking. So, you pull over and decide to be the one nice driver out there who will give this girl a ride home. She smiles, gets in, and thanks you for pulling over. You start to ask questions, trying to figure out who she is and why she is standing beside the road so late at night. She gives few answers, just muttering that she had been out dancing. She gives some directions to where she says she lives, but the directions seem strange, moving her further away from homes. Suddenly, she shouts, insisting that you pull over. You pull over, frightened, startled by the sudden determination in her voice. As you pull the car to a stop, you look around and notice that you are parked in front of a large cemetery. You turn around to ask your passenger what she means by telling you to pull over and let her out in this place, and, to your surprise, the girl has vanished completely.

Nearly every culture in the civilized world has one. They are known as "vanishing hitchhiker" stories. Many of them bear the same hallmarks, whether the story is from the rural southern United States or London and other parts of Europe. They always involve a road, sometimes in a city and sometimes not, that is frequented by drivers and vehicles. The driver stops and picks up what appears to be a lonely hitchhiker, most often a woman, who appears to be lost or in some need of assistance. The kind driver pulls over and lets them into the vehicle and asks for directions. At some point during the journey, the driver is asked to pull over, and when he or she turns to look at the passenger to ask why they should pull over, seemingly in the middle of nowhere, they find that their passenger has vanished. Sometimes this is followed by the driver investigating the nearby homes and finding out that the person who was in their car died along that road, or near the spot where they were asked to pull over, in some kind of horrible traffic accident or crime. In Chicago, there are a few of these stories, but the one that is most famous and most talked about is known as Resurrection Mary.

The Resurrection in this case often refers to Resurrection Cemetery on Archer Avenue in an area on the southwest side of the city of Chicago called Justice, Illinois. The story behind Mary has baffled residents and ghost hunters alike for decades. While many choose to dismiss the tales as just that, the fact is that so many people have supposedly seen Mary, even just glimpses of her, that many think there may be something to this legend. What's interesting is not only the number of people who have seen the supposed ghost of Mary, but the number of seemingly very sane and very credible people who have seen her.

The story that is most often connected to Chicago's Resurrection Mary is that she was a young girl who, one night, put on her best dress and headed out for a night of dancing. She reportedly went dancing that night at the nearby O'Henry Ballroom, an establishment still in existence today. Most of the time, the telling of this story says that it happened in the 1930s, although some suggest that it happened much earlier in the century.

The story is that she went to the ballroom with her boyfriend. Reportedly, the girl and her boyfriend danced the night away. However, at some point, the two of them had a huge fight. Mary decided that she would rather walk home in the cold and dark than ride with the boyfriend she was now furious with. The legend says that she left the O'Henry Ballroom in a huff, walking up Archer Avenue in the dark. Beside the road, the darkness reaching out for her on either side of the dimly lit street made it nearly impossible for her to see. Sure enough, another car eventually came along, and the driver, perhaps distracted, and maybe from the same ballroom she had just left, or possibly having just made a mistake while driving, strikes Mary. She is flung to the side of the road, her young life ended. Her grieving parents pay for a funeral, burying her in her best dress, and lay her to rest at Resurrection Cemetery, not far from the ballroom and from where she met her untimely demise in the first place.

A man named Jerry Palus, a resident of Chicago's south side, would later tell a story that would take things even further. He said that he went out to a dance hall known as the Liberty Grove and Hall located at 47th and Mozart. He claimed that, while there, he met a beautiful young girl. They danced the night away, and even kissed. Then, as the night grew late, she asked if Palus would give her a ride home. He agreed, hoping that he might get her phone number and call her again some time. She gave him directions to Archer Avenue, begging him to stop the car when they reached the gates of Resurrection Cemetery. Puzzled, Palus pulled over. In his version of the story, the woman got out of the car and ran around the front of it, heading for the iron gates that mark the entrance to the cemetery. As he watched, astonished, she reached the gates and then simply faded out of existence, vanishing into the darkness as if she had never been. That incident happened, reportedly, in 1939.

With Mary, she need not show up just at the O'Henry Ballroom. In fact, she has allegedly made appearances at various clubs and dance halls all over the south side of Chicago. In 1973, there is a story that Mary made an appearance at a night club called Harlow's, located on the southwest side of the city. Again, she is reported to have danced and was seen with men. She'd ask for a ride home, and then vanish when the car approached Resurrection Cemetery.

Also, in 1973, a cab driver was reported to have tried giving Mary a ride home. He approached the cemetery only to have his fare vanish. He reportedly pulled over and walked into Chet's Melody Lounge, a club directly across the street from Resurrection Cemetery. When he walked in, puzzled and angry, he asked if anyone had seen a young woman enter the club. He was furious that she had just walked out on his fare.

When she is seen and when people pick her up and attempt to drive her home, they insist that she seems real. There have been those who have danced with her and touched her. Those who have, say that her skin is cold to the touch, but that she seems normal and friendly. Only when they reach the cemetery entrance do things get particularly strange.

The gates of the cemetery allegedly bear the marks of Mary. The front gate has two metal iron bars that are clearly seen to be bent, and the paint has been chipped away from them. Legend has it that Mary herself made these marks, burning her hand prints into the metal while standing at the gates, watching as traffic passed. The cemetery says that the damage was done by a truck. Regardless, the bent iron bars are still there, having never been replaced.

Sometimes Mary is seen within the cemetery itself. Many who drive along Archer Avenue claim to see a girl, sometimes described as white in appearance, standing inside the cemetery. Some claim to see her standing at the gate, clutching those mysterious bars.

Mary is still being seen and reports still come in. In 1979, another cab driver, purportedly named Ralph, claims to have run into her. Ralph told a reporter from the *Suburban Trib* that he picked up a young and beautiful blond woman one night. He claimed the woman was very young, at the most 21 years of age, and compared her in age to his daughter. He said that she got into the back of his cab and sent him down the familiar Archer Avenue. Suddenly, he related, she jumped in the seat as if shocked and told him to pull over. He hit the brakes, slamming the car to a stop, and looked around, puzzled, since there was no house anywhere in sight. When he asked her which house she meant, she is said to have pointed ominously at the cemetery and then vanished right before his eyes. She did not open the door and she made no other sound. She was simply gone.

The reporter who took the story said that Ralph did not seem crazy. If anything, he seemed amazingly normal. The writer said that Ralph was about 57 years old and just as sane as anyone else. Ralph was reportedly a veteran, a father, and even coached a little league baseball team.

So, who is Resurrection Mary? Was she a real person? Is there any validity to the stories about her and her supposed death? No one can be certain, of course, but there have been attempts to tie the stories with any Marys buried in Resurrection Cemetery. There appear to be two potential candidates.

The person who most people think is actually Resurrection Mary is a young woman named Mary Bregovy. She fits the bill nicely, except that she had dark hair rather than the blond hair often described. Mary Bregovy was known to like dancing, was young, and died while out dancing with friends in 1934. That night she allegedly wore her best dress and went out, despite the fact that her parents had forbid her from doing so. According to friends, while she was out dancing, moving from one dance hall and club to another, she fell into a rough crowd of boys. She died in a car crash that night. The funeral director who embalmed her said he knew her from the neighborhood and that she was a nice girl. Her friends remembered her fondness for dancing and she was buried in an unmarked grave in Resurrection Cemetery. Local Chicago newspapers carried her obituary, complete with a photo.

In more recent years, Ursula Bielski, local Chicago author of many books about haunted locations in and around the city, claims that another possible candidate is a very young blond girl named Anna "Marija" Norkus. Her story is very similar to the tale, except that she was much younger when she died beside the road, hit by a car, and buried in the cemetery. Anna was said to have been born to Lithuanian parents and had a devotion to the Virgin Mary, so much so that she started to go by the name Maija, or Mary. Her love of dance led her father to take her to the O'Henry Ballroom for a night of music and dancing on her 13th birthday. This was thought to have been in July of 1927. As they drove home, at an intersection near Resurrection Cemetery, the car went off the road and into a deep railroad cut that could not be seen from the road. Anna was supposedly killed instantly.

Another possibility, also forwarded by Bielski, is that Resurrection Mary was a girl named Mary Miskowski. This Mary was said to be from the south side of Chicago. The tale told with her name is that she was out one night and fatally hit by a car as she crossed the street. In this version, she was dressed for a Halloween party.

Other versions of the story involving Mary are of cars driving down Archer Avenue and suddenly seeing a young girl dart out from the cemetery into the street. Several people, both men and women, say that they are certain they saw the girl and are certain that they hit her. Except that when they get out of their cars to check the damage, they find no body and they find nothing wrong with their car.

Incidents continue to occur. It seems that Resurrection Mary still haunts drivers into the new century. She has become a legend, almost beloved, in the Chicago area. Whether or not she ever existed, and whether or not she still haunts Archer Avenue, in and around the infamous Resurrection Cemetery, is a mystery to this day.

Rosehill Cemetery

Just about every city of some age has a cemetery that residents think is haunted. We have already discussed the long-abandoned cemetery known as Bachelor's Grove and how it has become famous beyond the borders of Chicago to ghost hunters everywhere. However, like most large urban areas, there are more cemeteries than just Bachelor's Grove in Chicago. What's more, there are more old cemeteries and some of them are still very active. You can pretty much see the entire history of the surrounding community by looking at the headstones and the markers on the graves at cemeteries like Rosehill Cemetery, located on Chicago's north side.

Even if you decide to come to Chicago and visit Rosehill and you are not looking for ghosts, the cemetery is spectacular. For some reason, over the years that it has been in existence, the cemetery has become an amazing collection of some of the most elaborate markers and headstones. Since the cemetery was first opened in 1859, it has amassed a huge number of famous and infamous people, making it a kind of celebrity cemetery for the city of Chicago.

Eighteen of Chicago's former mayors are buried there, which sets a record for any cemetery for sheer number of mayors in any cemetery anywhere. It is also the final resting place of a couple of Vice Presidents of the United States, as well as famous names like Hinckley and Schmitt. Even Oscar Mayer is buried there. Rosehill, combined with its companion cemetery near by, Graceland Cemetery, is very literally the who's-who of Chicago history.

The cemetery gates are ornate to begin with. When you approach the entrance to Rosehill, it looks like you are approaching a castle. There is a vast stone archway that extends some distance from the gate, complete with towers and small arched windows. One of those towers even has a bell in it. It looks, very much, like the famous Chicago Water Tower, located in downtown Chicago on Michigan Avenue, and one of the few structures to completely survive the Great Chicago Fire. Of course, that stands to reason as both the Water Tower and the gate to Rosehill were designed by William H. Boyington.

The cemetery itself got its name in a way that can only be found in a city like Chicago. Essentially, it was a clerical error. The man who owned the land that Chicago wanted to turn into one of its largest cemeteries was a farmer named Hiram Roe. He refused to sell the land unless the city promised to name the resulting cemetery after him. This was agreed upon and the cemetery was named "Roe's Hill." However, when the County Clerk entered the name to register it, he made a mistake and listed it as Rosehill, and the rest, as they say, is history.

25

Since the cemetery has so many famous Chicagoans, it is a tourist attraction for that reason alone. However, the architecture surrounding the markers and headstones is another reason. Some of the most elaborate markers you are likely to find are located in Rosehill. For example, there is a huge seventy-two-foot tall obelisk, like something you would see in Egypt or Washington, D.C., that is the gravesite of former Chicago Mayor John Wentworth. Wentworth was mayor of Chicago for two terms in the 1800s. He was also a very tall man for the time, standing six-foot, six-inches. He insisted that he have the tallest monument in Rosehill and he put up the $38,000 that was required to build the obelisk and got his wish. It is still the tallest structure in the cemetery.

Then there is the marker for Charles Hull. He was the man who gave his huge house to a woman named Jane Addams. She would found "Hull House," catering to the city's poor and become a major force for social change in the city of Chicago. When Hull died, he was buried beneath himself. Above his grave is a detailed statue of Hull sitting in a chair.

Then there is the monument for the man named George S. Bangs. His name may be lost to history, but the effects of what he did are still in existence to this day. He revolutionized the postal system by inventing a way to transport mail using railroad stations and rail cars, inventing something that was, at that time, called "fast mail." His tombstone consists of a huge tree, carved in stone, beside which an elaborate and detailed model of a mail car is seen disappearing into a train tunnel.

There is the tomb of Darius Miller. He was one of the people who helped uncover the Tomb of King Tut. His mausoleum looks very much like something you might find guarding the tomb of some unknown Pharaoh. In fact, his tomb is a scale model replica of the Temple of Anubis that you could find in Egypt.

The list of tombs goes on and on. Seeing the many statues and bizarre and ornate tombstones makes visiting and walking through Rosehill Cemetery a surreal experience, to say the least. What really makes Rosehill famous, however, are the ghost stories that go along with so many of those ornate tombstones. Apparently, being interred at the Rosehill Cemetery, no matter how famous or powerful you were in your life, is not enough to bring eternal rest. Many of those buried beneath those ornate stones still reportedly roam the grounds to this very day.

Boyington's Child

Let's start with the elaborate gates. It has become legend that even the gates are haunted. Boyington himself is buried just inside them, right next to one of his masterpieces. However, the legend is that his young

daughter, when he was building the ornamental and spectacular gates to the cemetery, liked to come and play inside the towers. She would often be seen peering out from one of the small arched windows, watching the traffic go by. Just a year after the cemetery gates were completed, she died of pneumonia. Reportedly, those walking by the cemetery gates at night sometimes still look up to the small window beneath the bell tower and see the face of a little girl peering back at them. They say it is the daughter of Boyington.

Richard Sears

Inside the cemetery is the intricate crypt containing the remains of Richard Sears, the man who started the Sears Company that has called Chicago and the Chicago area home for decades. The mausoleum looks like something you might find in ancient Greece, with elaborate columns and etched out of white stone. It even has an entrance directly from the street. Purportedly, however, Sears himself still walks the ground outside his crypt. Those who claim to have seen him report that he is often seen walking around the corner, headed towards his business rival and friend, A. Montgomery Ward.

Mary Shedden

Not all of the ghost stories are just among the famous and powerful who rest beneath the green lawns of Rosehill. One of the more famous graves is that of Mary Shedden. Shedden was supposedly poisoned by her husband back in 1931. She was laid to rest in Rosehill, but some say that if you look at the gravestone above her resting place, you will notice something strange. There appears to be two images of Mary within the stone that was carved for her. One image is of Mary when she was young and alive and smiling. However, just behind that is allegedly an image of Mary's grinning skull. Some say it is just an optical illusion created by the stone used to make the monument, but others are certain that they see the skull and that it is Mary Shedden herself grinning back at them from beyond the grave.

Lincoln Park Masonic Lodge Monument

Located within the cemetery is a bizarre monument erected by the Masons. It is known as a the Lincoln Park Masonic Lodge Monument.

The strange tales about this one involve the group that bought and maintained the monument in the first place. They had their charter revoked when rumors began to spread that they were conducting rituals in the black arts and dabbling in black magic. The monument itself is strange, containing a huge stone globe that, at times, has been known to fall off the monument and crash to the ground, rolling a bit and creating damage. Could this be because of the dark forces that the Masons dabbled in?

Lulu Fellows

Another monument of interest to ghost hunters belongs to the very tragic, and all-too young Lulu Fellows. She died in 1833 at only 16 years of age. Her monument is like many in Rosehill and bears a statue of the person buried beneath. Lulu's is that of a young girl, and now that statue is encased in glass to protect it from the harsh weather that often sweeps through Chicago. People who visit and find her grave often leave coins, small toys, flowers, and other mementos for her. It is said that you can smell fresh flowers at her grave, even in the middle of winter, when there are no flowers around or that are able to grown anywhere near the grave.

Frances Pearce

Then there is the infamous grave of Frances Pearce. Her story, like so many in the cemetery, is one of tragedy. She was a beloved mother and wife who died very young and, to top it off, her baby daughter died with her. Her husband was reportedly devastated when she passed. He had a statue placed upon her grave that was a sculpture of Frances laying back, holding her baby. This statue is also encased in glass — again, to protect it from the harsh Chicago winters and anyone who might be tempted to chip off a piece as a souvenir.

Now, however, the glass case has become part of the legend. The tale says that on the anniversary of the deaths of Frances and her baby daughter, a glowing mist fills the enclosure, as if the two have returned, looking for their husband and father outside the cold glass.

Elizabeth Archer

Frances' grave is not the only monument to profound tragedy. Down the way is the grave of Elizabeth Archer, who died in the 1950s, killing herself when the man she loved, Arnold Fischel, died. Reports are that Elizabeth can be found, looking lost and alone and scared, wandering the grounds of the cemetery near her grave.

Her love was so great that her father had a monument built for the both of them known as the Archer-Fischel Monument. It is here that Elizabeth is often seen, apparently still seeking and looking for the man she loved so much that she could not imagine living without him.

Darius Miller

Then there is the mystery behind the grave of Darius Miller. He was the one who helped uncover the tomb of King Tut. Of course, many legends have been spread that those who uncovered the tomb of the boy king have been cursed. Since Miller was there when the tomb was opened, it is thought that he did not escape that curse. The spring after he was there to see the tomb opened, he died under strange circumstances and he came to rest at Rosehill, in the tomb that resembles the one erected in Egypt to Anubis. Now, however, the legend is that every May 1, in the early morning hours, a blue light will shine brightly, piercing the sky, shining through the darkness, emanating from his tomb. Experts have been unable to come up with a reason for the strange blue light, but ghost hunters say that it is Miller's spirit, still restless and angry that he was taken by the curse.

Charles Hopkinson,

Another tale is that of the ghost of Charles Hopkinson, a real estate tycoon. He made money selling and buying real estate during the Civil War. When he died, his estate paid a famous architect to design and build an enormous crypt for him that would resemble a small Gothic cathedral. Those who owned plots around the proposed crypt said that this was unfair and would block the view of the graves of their loved ones and the court case made it all the way to the Illinois Supreme Court. The court decided in Hopkinson's favor. However, having such a large crypt seems to have not given the real estate man any comfort. Now it is said that on the anniversary of his death, you can stand near the crypt and hear soft, but sad and miserable moaning, followed by the rattling of chains.

It seems that there are as many tales of ghosts and haunts in Rosehill Cemetery as there are graves. One things is for sure, there are few cemeteries like Rosehill anywhere else in the world. That stands to reason, as there are few cities that are anything like Chicago. It seems that an odd, but complex, cemetery, filled with haunts, spirits, and demons, is the perfect accompaniment for a city as ornate, strange, and interesting at Chicago.

Ghosts of Flight 191

On May 25, 1979, it was warm and sunny in the Chicago area. O'Hare Airport was busy, like it always was, with planes taking off and landing, and the hundreds of thousands of passengers heading in and out of the airport were heading to destinations located around the world. One of the flights scheduled for that day was American Airlines Flight 191. It was just another flight, and this one was headed from O'Hare to Los Angeles. The air was clear, the sky blue, and there was a light northeast wind blowing across the tarmac when Flight 191, a McDonnell Douglas DC-10, pushed away from the gate. All things said, it had the appearance of a normal, uneventful take-off. However, as many people who study these things know, Flight 191 was about to make history as one of the worst airline disasters in the history of the United States.

On board the plane were 258 passengers and 13 crew members. All of them were settled back into their seats as the plane taxied down the runway. The plane reached its designated runway and powered up. Nervous passengers clung to their seat rests as the engines went from a dim whine to a steady roar. The plane rumbled and bounced its way down the runway.

What happened next happened very fast. The plane reached its critical take-off speed and the nose lifted off the ground. At that moment the right engine suddenly sheered away from the wing. Smoke trailed from the damaged wing; but inside the cockpit, everything that *could* go wrong *was* going wrong. The pilots, in the midst of the take-off, had no idea what had happened, but the plane was now veering wildly, tilting sideways to its left, the side now missing the engine pointing straight to the ground. The other engine screamed, trying to compensate for the lost engine; the pilots fought the controls, trying to bring the plane back to level, in hopes of circling around and landing again at the airport, but it was hopeless. The plane went into a stall and the huge plane plummeted to the earth.

The plane managed to rise a few hundred feet into the air. It was visible over the roof of the airport, enough so that one passerby could take a photo of the struggling plane, tilted to its side, smoke trailing from the damaged wing. Then it crashed just past the end of the runway into a field located across a major road; it barely missed the huge field of oil tanks used by an oil company. The tip of the left wing hit the ground, carving a trench into the grass of the field across the road from the airport. The rest of the plane quickly followed, turning end over end for a moment before the plane ripped into pieces. Jet fuel and debris flew, a spark ignited the fumes and the fuel, and the remains of the plane exploded into flames. It struck a shed used by construction workers, who were working on a nearby project. Inside that shed were two workers who never had a chance.

The plane became a fireball. The fuselage broke into pieces, scattering debris, seats, paper, metal, and human remains across the empty field, barely missing the trailer park that resided there. All 258 passengers and crew were killed and the two on the ground brought the total number of deaths to 273. To this day, it remains the deadliest accidental crash in the history of the United States. It is still the second accidental crash in the history of the world involving a DC-10 aircraft, just behind a Turkish Airlines flight 981 that crashed in March of 1974 in France, taking with it 346 lives.

An investigation into the craft revealed, at first, one possible culprit and then another. At first, the crash was blamed on a small metal pin that was used to hold the engine on to the wing. It was found amidst the wreckage and shown to be broken. In the beginning, it was thought that it was this defective part that caused the accident, and since this was a part used on many DC-10s around the world, the FAA soon grounded all DC-10s in the country. However, investigators probed deeper and found the real reason the plane went down was shoddy maintenance.

It had become standard practice to repair the engines via a method that did not completely remove the engine. The practice, instead, put increased pressure and weight on the pin that ultimately broke. Stress fractures formed in the pin that held the engine on from repeated use of this method. That stress was particularly strong during take-offs and landings, and on that day in May, the stress fractures reached a breaking point. The pin sheered in half and the engine went. When it fell, it tore out hydraulic lines and other key components that kept the plane in the air. The pilots, at the same time, overcompensated and fought the controls, unaware of just how badly damaged their plane was. They tried to slow down. Had they just increased their speed, there was a slight chance the plane would have come out of its stall, leveled off, and it may have been able to circle around. However, they eventually reached a reduced speed that was too low for the plane to handle and it went down.

It was a horrible tragedy that completely stunned the city. For weeks, the local news was filled with stories of the investigation into the tragedy. It took years, but eventually a memorial was erected to remember those who died on Flight 191. It should have been the end of it. O'Hare eventually went back to normal. New flight standards were issued and DC-10s were eventually cleared. The way in which the engines were repaired on the planes was changed and DC-10s were ultimately allowed to fly again. Normal.

Except, that is, for the people who live in the trailer park next to the field where the plane went down and almost 300 people lost their lives. For some of them, it seems, the saga of Flight 191 still goes on and on and on—because the passengers on Flight 191, at least in some cases, are not entirely at rest.

For residents in the trailer park, one of the first things they reported were strange lights and sounds coming from the field next door to where they lived. Sounds of moaning and crying are said to be heard, as well. Residents' dogs seemed to notice that something was stirring there, as many reported that their animals would bark in the direction of the field. People thought, at first, that these were flashlights being used by grisly souvenir seekers. However, whenever anyone investigated, they found the fields empty. The police and other authorities were called to report people trespassing on the property and many police and fire officials *did* respond to those calls. Allegedly, they always found the field empty.

Other residents have reported hearing footsteps on the grounds outside their homes. Sometimes these footsteps even mount the small stairs leading to the doors of these houses. Then comes the knock. For some residents, when they open the door, they find their porches empty. In at least one case, a resident opened the door and found a man standing there. He was wearing out-of-date clothes, from the late '70s, and looked lost. He even spoke, saying he was lost and late and needed to use a phone. When the resident turned to grab the phone, they found the man had disappeared.

For many residents, the knocking and turning of their doorknobs happened in the hours and days just after the crash, but to this day residents claim that they still experience this. Sometimes they hear the knocking on their windows. Sometimes it seems like the person is trying to open their front doors and come right in.

One resident reportedly opened their door and found a man standing there. Again, he was wearing old-fashioned clothes. This man said that he had lost his luggage and needed to make a connection, and that he needed to make a phone call. Again, as the resident tried to help, the man just vanished.

In another case, a man who lived in the area was out walking his dog near the trailer park one night. From out of the darkness, a young man emerged. He approached the man walking his dog, again, looking lost and out of sorts, dressed in late-'70s clothing. The man walking his dog also said the young man who approached him smelled like gasoline and appeared to be smoldering. He asked the dog walker where he could find a phone, because he had an emergency call to make. The puzzled walker knew that there was a public phone not far away, just behind him, having passed it minutes before. He turned to point to the phone and then turned back to see if he could help the man further, only to find himself alone on the street with his dog.

Many residents moved out of the trailer park after the accident. They took their tales of the strange noises, their worried pets, and the men on the porch asking for phones with them. However, as new people moved into the park, they too reported strange sights and sounds and more reports of people knocking on the windows and turning the doorknobs surfaced. The reports continue to this day.

Even the airport itself supposedly has a ghost that many believe is connected to Flight 191, although no one can be sure. In the terminal, many state seeing a man using a phone booth dressed in outdated clothing—clothing more common among travelers in the late '70s. People walking around him are puzzled by the strange-looking and strangely-dressed man. Many who continue to watch him are amazed when he simply vanishes, disappearing into the ether, perhaps eternally catching his fatal flight.

What's more, relatives who had their loved ones die on Flight 191 say that they have seen apparitions, as well. And the residents of the trailer park and those who live near the crash site, to this day, say that they still see, hear, and even smell things that should not be and are out of place for what is still an empty field.

Is one of the worst tragedies to ever occur near Chicago still going on for the sad and desperate passengers of Flight 191? Of course, there are skeptics who credit overactive imaginations and residents who may have had too much to drink from time to time. But the stories continue and those telling the stories are not only residents, but also police and firemen and those many respect, whose credibility is flawless. It remains, of course, a mystery to this day.

Part Two
Missing People

It happens all the time. The sad and scary fact of life is that sometimes people just disappear. Most of the time, the people who vanish are found. Many times they are found dead, having been murdered. Sometimes, however, they are just never seen again. Despite the efforts of family, friends, and authorities, it's like the person has vanished into thin air. Many believe that, in those cases, there is still a reasonable explanation for why the people vanished. Sometimes people believe that extraterrestrial or other strange reasons are the answer. The fact remains, however, that sometimes people just vanish and no one knows where they went.

While these things happen all over the world and there is no specific location that is more prone to vanishing individuals than others, and despite what conspiracy theorists would have you believe, the fact is that the more people cluster together in large urban areas, the more likely it is that these cases will be reported. It's easy to get lost amidst the crush of people, and one of the first things you learn when living in a city is that you keep to yourself and you don't get involved in things that do not concern you. It is entirely possible to live in an urban environment, when your neighbor is practically within touching distance, and never see or speak to them. Thus, when someone vanishes, they just disappear and no one is the wiser.

Chicago is not different. There are a number of stories about people who have disappeared throughout the history of the city. Many of them were probably the result of criminal activities, but there are some that continue to baffle police and frustrate the families involved. At any time, these crimes could be solved by finding a key clue or discovering a body, or anything that might provide the final piece of evidence that leads authorities to the location of a body—or to wherever the person may have vanished. In the meantime, however, each of these remains a mystery, with real people, real families looking, hoping, and wishing for clues or an answer.

Chapter Three
John Spira

For residents of the western suburbs of Chicago, the name of John Spira is a familiar one. That's because, for a long time, there were two huge billboards in the Chicagoland area bearing his name, giving his description, and discussing the fact that he has been missing since February of 2007. Of course, now, that sign has been torn down, and the business that John owned and operated has been burned to the ground. He is still being sought by his family, however. His biggest champion, his sister, Stephanie, lives in Arizona and still manages the website and other online methods she is using to search for her brother. Despite their best efforts, John's family continues to be frustrated by the efforts of police, who still consider John's case to be a missing persons case and not a murder.

John was a man who was exciting in personality, if not stature. While small in height and frame, he presented himself as larger than life and full of fun, as described by his friends and family. He ran a contracting business, doing construction work, for years in the nearby Chicago western suburbs in the county of DuPage. His business was successful, but he also had a passion for music. John was known as "Chicago Johnny" and he played blues music in and around various clubs in the Chicago area and suburbs. On the day that he went missing, he was 45 years old. He had brown hair, hazel eyes, and weighed about 165 pounds, standing five-foot-eight-inches tall.

For John's family, the general lack of concern and response from authorities has fueled their continued frustration. The authorities have suggested that John may have killed himself. His family, however, says that this is ridiculous. If that were the case, why has no body been found? One investigator pointed out that someone who had committed suicide cannot bury or burn their body once the act has been completed. Also, why had he made plans the night he vanished, if he'd just planned to take his own life later that same evening? Then again, very little makes much sense about John's disappearance.

The strange circumstances surrounding his vanishing has puzzled family and investigators for years. The lack of evidence and anything that authorities could use to further the case leading to an arrest has added to the frustration. It seems as if John Spira simply vanished from the face of the earth on February 23, 2007.

That day appeared to be a normal day for all involved in the life of John. In fact, he had plans to meet up with a friend for dinner that night. It was a typical day at the office for him. Once the sun began to set, he made a phone call (at 7:09 p.m.), reportedly from his desk at his office to a friend he was going to meet for dinner. The plan was to meet up with that friend for dinner at 8:30 p.m. in the suburb of Oak Brook. His friend was there at the restaurant where they had planned to meet at that time. John was the type who usually showed up on time or early, and he never arrived. He never called. Neither was typical for John. The mystery of what happened to John Spira lies in what happened to him between the time he left his office and when he was supposed to be meeting up with his friend for dinner.

One of the key figures in the vanishing of John Spira was his business partner, David Stubben. John and David ran the Universal Cable Construction company. He was the last person to see John alive, as reported by at least two other people. He told investigators that nothing strange had happened that night and that he had spoken to John, his partner for twenty years, that night in the parking lot of the construction company that they had operated for years. He told investigators that he had no idea what happened to John, and has since disputed whether or not he was the last person to see John alive.

John's car never left the parking lot behind the building where John and David worked. This was strange, since John normally parked the truck, a company vehicle, in front of the office building. Given the time frame involved, that means John must have vanished sometime between 7:10 p.m. and about 7:45 p.m.

Suspicion tends to lie with two people. It turned out that John and his wife were in the midst of a contentious divorce. It had been going on for some time, two years, on the day he vanished. That morning, he had just finalized an agreement that would have settled the divorce and divided up their property and goods. However, once John vanished, his wife said that they had not yet reached an agreement and that nothing had been signed or filed that morning. She was also hesitant to file a missing persons report when it became obvious that John had disappeared and was not going to be showing up again anytime soon.

Also cast under a pall of suspicion was John's business partner, Stubben. Accusations that Stubben and John's wife were more than just passing friends have been thrown about. Although Stubben was the last person to see John alive, he insists that John was still alive and well when he left the parking lot of the construction company. However, he has staunchly refused to take a lie detector test during the time since John vanished.

Strange things have continued to happen in and around John Spira and his disappearance. When his family erected their banner near the offices that John and Stubben used to run their business, the business itself was leveled in a fire. Nothing remained of the offices of UCC except charred pieces of debris. Then, not long after, the banner/billboard bearing John's face was burned and destroyed, as well.

In addition to the two huge billboards, John's family erected a huge 20' x 5' banner, anchored to the ground, in September of 2007. Just two days after the banner was put up, the building where the two men had worked caught fire, and the banner was gone. The sign had been erected directly across the street from the UCC offices. When the fire departments from neighboring communities arrived to put out the fire, they spent time waiting before they could approach the building because, inside, numerous rounds of ammunition were going off, creating a life-threatening hazard to firefighters.

According to Stephanie McNeil, David Stubben has accused John and Stephanie of setting the fire. He has also reportedly changed his story about when he last saw John and where he was when he saw him. Another strange occurrence is that a sheet of heavy-duty plastic sheeting was missing from John's office. It was definitely enough plastic sheeting to wrap a body.

As for the police, they still staunchly refuse to acknowledge that John Spira is anything but a missing person. They refuse to turn the case into a murder investigation. They say they have no body. They have no evidence to support that John was murdered. Without that body, and without a declaration that John is dead, there is no reason to switch from a missing person to a murder investigation.

The DuPage County police say that the case is still open. In August of 2011, Stephanie McNeil was back in Chicago handing out fliers on a Chicago street in hopes that someone might recognize John and be able to provide information. She wants the case to become a homicide investigation and get out of the realm of missing persons. She told the press that it is a nightmare; every time the phone rings or a body is found in and around the Chicago area, she hopes that it is her brother and that, at last, her worries and concerns can be put to rest. So far, that is still just a dream and she is still searching.

Police acknowledge that someone made a phone call from John's office after he had allegedly made his final phone call to his friend about meeting for dinner. However, police say that they do not have any information, or leads, regarding who made that phone call or why.

Stephanie McNeil makes a yearly trip back from Phoenix, Arizona to the Chicago area. She says she will not rest until John is able to rest and bristles when the police insist that it is still a missing persons case.

She says she knew, from the moment she heard about it, that John was dead because John would not just vanish — John had too many things going for him to just up and disappear like that.

Stephanie McNeil has made roughly 15 trips back to Chicago since she moved to Phoenix, by her estimation. She says she comes back to make sure that John's case stays active and alive, conducting searches, handing out fliers, and making appearances in the local press venues. She has done what she can to get the word out about John's disappearance, including getting his story featured on ID Discovery, on a show called *Disappeared* that features stories of the missing.

To add to the strangeness, in 2010, the ex-wife of John Spira, Suzanne, was found dead in her apartment in New York. John's sister said to the press that she only learned about it when a friend of Suzanne's mentioned it to her, and she did not hear about it from the police. What Suzanne Spira may have known about her ex-husband's disappearance and/or death will never be known now. This is a thought that angers Stephanie McNeil, as is the way the DuPage County authorities have treated her and her family.

In 2011, McNeil filed a Freedom of Information Act appeal to get all of the records that DuPage County authorities have about her brother's investigation. Despite the filing, DuPage authorities have refused to turn over the paperwork, insisting that it is part of an ongoing investigation. McNeil has taken the matter to court to try and get the information. She eventually filed a petition with the Attorney General's office to get the paperwork and the Attorney General ordered DuPage County to hand over the papers. McNeil soon found herself in possession of an inch-and-a-half thick bundle of paperwork, despite the fact that she knows, having seen it, that there was still much more that was not released.

Stephanie McNeil helped write this chapter and, as part of discussions with the author, sent the following information via email, that was part of her blog where she keeps John's case alive:

> I have finally gone through the 1.5 inches of paper that was sent to me by the police in response to my FOIA request. I don't think I have everything, but what I do have I find interesting. The police have done much more than I thought they had. That said, there was much that wasn't done or simply glanced over. For instance, I don't believe the use of John's credit card in September and December of 2007 was thoroughly checked out. The account had been closed since 2002. Dave Stubben was an authorized user. The documents I received don't reflect much investigation on that issue, in fact none at all.
>
> Also, on 3/7/07, Dave Stubben was asked several times if John had been using company funds for John's other adventures or if John had

been taking money from the business. Dave said no. He also confirmed that "there were no serious concerns about the business which would have driven John away."

Fran Armstrong, the office manager, said nothing was askew, basically. In fact, Fran stated on 3/1/07, that there were no unaccounted company checks or withdraws from the company accounts.

Fran was interviewed again on June 22, 2007, and indicated "that she had knowledge of all the financial matters and could not think of any suspicious activity on either John or Dave's part." Both John's personal accountant and business accountant found no financial issues. The police report notes that "[Dave] went from saying he did not pay much attention to the financial matters and said Fran would be able to tell us about them, to saying he had been watching the money issue for some time now." That was in March. Then, in September, after the fire, suddenly, Dave says John amassed over $1M in debt (NOT!), had several failed businesses (NOT), and that John was taking money from the business (wouldn't he have known that in March as he'd been watching the finances "for sometime now?"). Further, during the time between John's disappearance in February and around the time of the fire in September, John's employees seemed to have become experts on John's personal finances. How'd that happen? Did they do their own personal investigation? Did they speak with John's accountant? Or did Dave start spinning facts to his employees after John disappeared?

Dan Maupin, a UCC employee, flatly accused John of embezzlement. Another employee at the Harvey office, whose husband works at the West Chicago office, told police that her husband said John borrowed money from some "bad people." How the hell would this guy know that? Does he know the "bad people"? Was he there when John made this supposed deal? Why wasn't he investigated? He must have some information on these "bad people"; either that, or it's an irresponsible half-ass statement made by someone who is completely ignorant of the facts. Who is feeding these people this information? Maybe it is true [and] maybe John was embezzling money from the company. I hate to think that's true, but if it is, that would seem to be a motive for a business partner to be awfully angry. And if it isn't, then it's pure slander meant to put the blame on John for his disappearance in order to remove the focus from the obvious culprit here. And if it's true, why then did Dave, Fran, and the business accountant say all was well financially when initially interviewed just after John's disappearance and as late as June, '07? I'd like to know what proof of embezzlement they have.

Something else I find interesting is that Dave knew the sign (the banner) was gone on Saturday, the day before the fire. That was news to me. What the police report states is as follows: "The sign was subsequently taken down by unknown individual(s) sometime on Saturday. Mr. Stubben also mentioned that he has been having problems with the owner of the new building at the corner of County Farm Road and St. Charles Road. Mr. Stubben indicated that the property owner (unknown name) had come into the business shouting at Fran one day. The owner feels that Mr. Stubben's property is an 'eyesore', and has given Mr. Stubben's employees a hard time about it on more than once occasion...."

Was Dave implying that the neighbor took the sign down? Did the employees confirm that the neighbor yelled at them? In the neighbor's interview with police, he indicated "he had not had any problems with the owners next door except for one time: their employees were using the first 15' to 18' off the road for parking. [He] addressed this issue with the owners and asked them to stop." So that would seem to contradict Dave's statement. It remains my belief that it burned up in the fire.

Here's something else that's interesting: Dave was contradicted by [two] other people about being the last one at the office with John on the night of his disappearance. Dave says he left after these [two] guys on Friday night, but they both say that when they left, Dave and John were still there, and one guy said when he left, only Dave and John were still there. It appears Dave is disputing he was the last one to see John, but the other [two] guys had no reason to lie. And another thing, Dave said when he left that night, John's truck (owned by UCC) was parked in the front lot. However, when the police went to the property on 2/26, the truck was parked in the back, locked and gated area, and had no snow underneath and, funny thing, was parked in the spot Dave always parks in. What a coincidence. Since there was no snow underneath it, it had to have been moved Friday night, the night of his disappearance, because it started snowing heavily that night. Dave had a financial interest in the truck and lo and behold, it's parked in the spot Dave habitually uses. And only a few employees have keys to the gate lock. Why would John have moved the truck to the back if he'd planned on going to Oak Brook? And why would he have parked it in Dave's usual spot? He wouldn't have.

Dave also stated on 3/9/07 that he had just "recently found out about John's pending divorce, even though it had been ongoing for the past 2 years." Later, he states the reason John and Dave had not been close friends for the past two to two and one half years was due to "Mr. Spira's extramarital activities, and the divorce that he and his wife Suzanne were going through. Mr. Stubben stated that the divorce was very bitter." So, Dave had just found out about the divorce and his extramarital affair around the time of John's disappearance and yet [it] was the cause of the breakdown of their friendship for the past 2 years? Huh? More spinning here? Seems as if he's trying to paint John in a bad light.

John and Suzanne were estranged [and] had been for 2 years...Why Dave thought John had to share this information with him is beyond me. These are personal, not business-related issues. I think the real cause of the breakdown was Dave. Here's what some others had to say about him:

"He advised Stubben was a meticulous person and had to have everything arranged his way and this caused a lot of arguments between Spira and Stubben. He further described Stubben as having a short temper...During one of the meetings...Stubben had an argument with [subject]... During the altercation, Stubben threw a cell phone at [subject] which caused a small laceration on [subject's] chin. [Subject] said Stubben drank a lot and was usually drunk by 3 p.m. After 8 months of this type of behavior, he decided to leave the company to seek employment elsewhere. He believed this all occurred in mid to late 2003.'"

The frustrations and anger that McNeil feels still continues, as does her determination and the investigation. So far, there is still no body. No one has been arrested in the case of John Spira. It remains a mystery.

41

Chapter Four
Stacy Peterson

Policemen and women form bonds that are legendary beyond the borders and walls of the local police station. Sometimes, the police force is referred to as a "fraternity," with cops watching the backs of their fellow officers. Police officers have been known to watch out for the families of their fellow policemen. The tales of cops helping other cops are legendary and well known. Police face things that the average human being would find so awful that they would be tempted to curl up in a ball if they ran into them on their own. Few people call the police unless they are at one of their own worst moments in their lives, which makes them oftentimes very unpleasant and unhappy to see the officers when they arrive. As such, it is often an us-versus-them feeling among cops, and they, naturally, draw their horses around each other for protection.

However, in the Chicago suburb of Bolingbrook, there is now a question as to just how far that protection and willingness to help might have gone. It is one thing to help out a police officer's family if the officer dies in the line of duty or has a brief lapse—it may be understandable how his fellow cops might want to cover for him. The question in Bolingbrook, however, is: Did the police force let a fellow officer get away with something more serious? For example, might it be that a former police sergeant in Bolingbrook murdered two of his wives?

Stacy Ann Cales was a beautiful, blond, young woman of 19 years of age when she married a Bolingbrook police sergeant named Drew Peterson in October of 2003. Peterson was a smooth talking sort of guy who was easily twice her age. Throughout his life, Peterson never had a problem getting women. Whatever his personality was really like, it seemed that he was effortlessly able to get gorgeous young women to fall for him. He had been married before and, in fact, his divorce from his previous wife, Kathleen Savio, had just been finalized on October 10, 2003. Stacy and Drew were married on October 18 that same year.

Before Savio, Peterson had been married to a woman named Victory Connolly. That marriage ended in divorce and accusations of abuse in 1992, after ten years of marriage. Before Connolly, Peterson had been married to Carol Brown, in a marriage that lasted from 1974 to 1980. Brown said she had had enough of Peterson's infidelity when she divorced him.

By all accounts Stacy was very much in love with Drew. Peterson had children from his past wives and Stacy did her best to try and make friends with them. She herself longed to have her own children and wanted Peterson to be the father. She even had discussions with Peterson's ex-wife, Kathleen Savio, prior to their marriage where she defended her decision to be with Drew. Reportedly, Savio attempted to warn Stacy away. In fact, though, Drew had begun his affair with Stacy before he initiated the divorce proceedings with Savio. Stacy would go on to tell a neighbor that Drew would invite her over to his house and sneak her into the basement to have sex while Savio slept upstairs in the same home.

Stacy and Drew were married and, before long, Stacy was pregnant. She gave birth to two children for Drew Peterson. This brought his number to four, as he had two children, both boys, with Kathleen Savio. The divorce proceedings with Kathleen, before the wedding, were contentious between Drew and Kathleen. In fact, their lives were chaotic and their lives did not get any less so after the divorce. Reports show that there were eighteen domestic disturbance calls to their homes between the years 2002 and 2004, sometimes for being late when returning the boys after a visitation. Things changed radically in March of 2004.

Drew had the boys for the weekend and was supposed to return them when Sunday came. He and the boys walked the short distance from where Drew and Stacy lived to where Kathleen lived. When they knocked, there was no answer. Drew summoned a neighbor and asked him to enter the home and see if Kathleen was inside. According to Drew Peterson, moments later, their neighbor yelled out and he ran upstairs to see what was wrong. Kathleen lay nude in the jacuzzi tub, dead. It was ruled that she drowned even though there was no water in the tub.

Whether or not this bothered Stacy is not entirely clear. However, it was evident to some who knew Stacy that the things Drew was asking of her were driving her crazy. He was insanely jealous, convinced at all times that she was running around with other men, younger men, and would call her constantly. When Stacy took a job as a kind of assistant to their next door neighbor, Drew did not take to it kindly. He felt that Stacy should stay home and take care of his house and his children and nothing else. He considered her not wanting to do the same as an insult. His obsessions with finding out where Stacy was increased, at times resulting in confrontations when he was found checking her cell phone, her emails, and then accusing her of sleeping with other men, including her brother-in-law.

Things were getting more and more tense. Stacy's life was spiraling out of control because she was constantly under the thumb of Drew Peterson. At a party, attended by the next door neighbor for whom Stacy

43

worked, Stacy told the neighbor that Drew had just pushed her into the television set. Violence between the two reportedly escalated.

Stacy eventually decided that she had had enough. She told Drew that he had to leave the house, and he did. She said she was going to initiate divorce proceedings and she promised to take him to the cleaners, providing for her and the children. Then, suddenly, on October 28, 2007, Stacy Peterson disappeared.

Drew told neighbors and friends that he'd gotten a call from Stacy saying that she had met another man. She said she was going to run off with this man, and that was what he claimed happened. He was not concerned about her safety, he said, because she had run off with another man.

Stacy had left another voice-mail message, for her father, about a week before she vanished. There was no indication that anything was wrong. It said:

> Hey, Dad! It's me, Stacy; I just wanted to call and tell you that I love you. I also wanted to give you my new phone number. Okay, love you.

Those were the last words ever heard from Stacy Peterson.

Stacy's family did not believe it. They knew that she was fond of Drew's two sons. They also knew that she was a good mother. It made no sense to them that she would just up and leave. It made no sense to them that she would not call and tell them what her plans were. Most of all, they did not remotely believe anything that Drew Peterson was telling them. They also didn't believe that his previous wife, Kathy, had died in a dry tub from drowning all on her own. Savio's family, as well, did not believe the official report and figured that Peterson had used his influence among the police force and other authorities to get away with murder. Now, with his fourth wife missing, the families combined to go to the press and start a search for Stacy.

Instead of helping with the search, Drew Peterson went on television. As the case garnered national attention, from the likes of Larry King and the *Today* show, Drew made appearances. Appearing smug, cracking jokes, laughing, and crying, he blamed the problems in his marriage squarely on Stacy, saying that her mood and her temper fluctuated based on her menstrual cycle. He claimed to have gotten her plastic surgery and other things to try to appease her, but that Stacy still demanded more. During one memorable appearance on the *Today* show, he even turned to the camera and pleaded with Stacy to return home.

The public was not buying it. A huge search was conducted for Stacy. Wooded and swampy areas near her Bolingbrook home were searched, all to no avail. It seemed as if she had vanished.

Peterson continued to make appearances on television. The local media set up outside his home, filming him coming and going. Peterson claimed to be annoyed by the attention, but also seemed to revel in it. Once, he showed up with his own video camera and filmed the media as they filmed him. He claimed he was a "jokester"and that he deeply missed Stacy, but that his way of dealing with it was by making jokes. He also claimed that he was not going to participate in any searches for Stacy because he knew that she was not in the woods, but had run off somewhere with another man.

The case took on comical proportions. Peterson appeared on a local radio show and even agreed to participate in a "Win a Date with Drew Peterson" contest. The radio station ultimately shot down the idea, but it did not endear Peterson with the public. Many were calling for him to be arrested, but the police said they had no body and they had no clear evidence that Peterson had done anything to Stacy.

At one point, it was revealed that Peterson had met another woman and had another girlfriend. Her name was Christina Raines and she worked at a local tanning salon where she met Drew. Meanwhile, Drew had hired a publicist in addition to high-priced lawyers. He also decided to retire from the police force, saying that the publicity from the searches was too much for him. He was now receiving a pension from the Bolingbrook police department, all the while the public was convinced he was a double murderer.

In 2009, Drew announced that he was now engaged to Raines. This would have made her his fifth wife. Raines was 23 years old at the time, much younger than Drew. Their case made national news when Raines' father appeared on the *Dr. Phil* show, begging him to help his daughter get away from Peterson. The two did split for a time, but in February 2009, Raines said they were back together and hoped to get married. She said Drew made her laugh.

Things got bad for Peterson. The case of his third wife, Kathleen Savio, was re-opened with all of the publicity surrounding the disappearance of Stacy. Eventually, Kathleen's body was exhumed and a second autopsy done. This time it was ruled a homicide and an arrest warrant was made for Drew Peterson. Peterson was arrested on a public street corner, quipping to the press that were there to see it happen that he "should have returned those library books."

Since Stacy disappeared, strange things have popped up from time to time. For example, Peterson's step-brother attempted suicide. When asked about it, he claimed that, at one point, he had been called over to the home by Drew because Drew needed help with something. He entered the home to find a 55-gallon blue barrel in the bedroom. He then helped Drew load that barrel into the back of a van. What Drew

45

did with the barrel, he did not know, but he became convinced he had helped Drew move the body and couldn't live with that thought. He then stated that he and Drew had once been in possession of a number of containers from a local cable company and even gave descriptions of them, thinking those could have been used to dispose of her body.

At one point, two truck drivers came forward saying that they thought Drew Peterson had approached them at a truck stop and offered them money to transport a large blue barrel. However, when police investigated their stories, they found that the two truckers had not even been in the area and that their stories did not hold water.

Drew's step-brother also stated that Drew had handed him Drew's own cell phone. He claimed that Drew held on to Stacy's phone and, at some point during the night when Stacy allegedly disappeared, Drew called his own phone using Stacy's cell.

Peterson has sat in jail and has yet to go on trial for the murder of Kathleen Savio (at this printing). The laws involved in murder cases were changed in Illinois to allow statements supposedly given by Savio, that if she ever vanished, it would be Drew that had caused her to do so, to be used in the trial against him. Since Savio is dead, and she apparently uttered these phrases to relatives, Drew's lawyers say this is hearsay. The legal battle has raged on, all the while Drew Peterson sits in a jail cell. One appeals court threw out the statements, and then the Illinois Supreme Court put them back in.

So far, no trace of Stacy Peterson has ever been found. Drew's children are now being raised by his oldest son, who also became a police officer. Stacy Peterson's family still hopes that Drew Peterson will finally tell them what happened and where their daughter is. Drew, meanwhile, still maintains the story that Stacy left him to run off with another man.

Perhaps, only time will tell.

Update:

Drew Peterson was eventually convicted of murdering his third wife, Kathleen Savio, in 2012 and is now in prison.

Chapter Five
Lisa Stebic

She was a beautiful, brunette, mother of two beautiful children. She was married to a man named Craig Stebic and they lived in a beautiful suburban home near Chicago. By all standards that modern man puts against a family, it seemed as if the Stebics had it all. Behind closed doors, however, many did not know that the lives of the Stebics were falling apart. Lisa and Craig were in the process of getting a divorce. Exactly how contentious the divorce was going to be is unknown, since we have only one side of the story to go on. The reason we have only one side of the story is that on April 30, 2007, Lisa Stebic simply vanished. Not a single sign of her has been seen nor heard since and her family believes that it was her husband who was behind her disappearance.

For a time, until the Drew Peterson story took center stage, the local news media was captivated as the search went on for Lisa Stebic. Her pretty features, with long brown hair hanging down on either side of her face, filled the television screens of thousands of Chicagoans. Eager news junkies gobbled up each revelation and wondered when Craig would be arrested and charged with a crime. Just like with the Drew Peterson case, the media camped outside the Stebic home, even sending news helicopters to hover over the Stebic backyard, catching images of Craig Stebic and his son and daughter frolicking in their backyard pool.

Then, in a turn so bizarre that there are few to this day who believe it could have happened, this story ended up nearly ending the career of one of the most popular female newscasters in the city.

The Stebics lived in one of the fastest-growing suburban areas in and around Chicago: Plainfield. Back in early '90s, a huge portion of that town was nearly wiped off the map by one of the worst tornadoes the city had ever seen. These days, however, the area is filled with housing developments and many young men and women set their claim in the area as the place to start their families with the dream of a new house, a yard, and a safe neighborhood now a reality. It was here that the Stebics moved.

Lisa Stebic, when she vanished, was 37 years old and stood a mere five-feet, two-inches tall. She weighed all of 120 pounds. She had brown hair and eyes and two tattoos visible to the average person. She had a small rose tattooed on her ankle and a large butterfly on her lower back.

According to Craig Stebic, his wife decided to run off with her boyfriend. The only thing that Lisa's family has found strange about that is that she left at her home money, keys, her cell phone, and other possessions that the average person would take with them if they were going somewhere. She has also never attempted to contact anyone. She has not called, sent a letter or email, or tried to contact her parents or anyone in her family. According to her family, this is completely unlike Lisa and goes against her character.

Lisa's family and friends have done what they can to keep Lisa in the forefront of people's minds. They have posted a $75,000 reward. They have also put up billboards and handed out fliers to numerous local businesses. They have held frequent candlelight vigils. At those vigils, there have been news crews and members of Lisa's family. There has been one very noticeable and strange absence at those vigils.

Craig Stebic has not appeared at a single one. He has also done virtually nothing to prevent the general public and the local media from continuing to target him as a person of interest and a likely suspect in her disappearance. Despite repeated pleas from Lisa's relatives, and encouragement from law enforcement, Craig Stebic has refused to take a polygraph. In fact, according to police, he has virtually stopped attempting to assist them at all. He has refused to appear on local media, for the most part. Initially, he seemed willing to talk, and then slowly retreated from any public speech about his missing wife. He has also refused to answer questions from law enforcement and remains a person of interest to the police. No sign of Lisa's body has ever been found, despite searches.

Amy Jacobson, meanwhile, was a popular and attractive television news reporter for WBBM television in Chicago, the local NBC affiliate. She was not an anchor, but the reporter the station sent out into the field to get the stories on the streets. She had attracted quite a following among fans of the local news broadcasts and was just one of many reporters who had taken up their camp outside the Stebic home, along with national news sources like *The Today Show* and *The Early Show*.

Exactly how it happened remains unclear. According to Jacobson, she was just trying to get as close to Craig Stebic as she could to get the story from him. She claims that she made a bad judgement call and got a little too casual and friendly with the man that most of the city suspected of murdering his wife and disposing of the body so completely that no one could find a trace of it. Craig Stebic, like he had been about his wife, has had nothing to say to the media about what happened and has remained silent.

One day, the local Chicago CBS affiliate sent their news helicopter to hover over the Stebic home. They were hoping to catch another shot of Craig Stebic in his backyard, perhaps, to have some additional footage to roll when they did story updates. As the helicopter hovered over the backyard, they got shots of Craig Stebic in the yard, as well as his kids in the pool. Then the cameraman noticed that there were additional kids in the pool and standing in the sliding glass door that led into the backyard was a face that the cameraman, and most of Chicago, recognized. It was Amy Jacobson in a white bikini top with a towel draped around her waist and hanging down over her legs.

Immediately, the local CBS affiliate cut into local programming with the news. The images of Jacobson in the bikini top ran across the city and, once again, made national headlines. NBC was forced to fire Jacobson, despite her apologies and protests that nothing was happening between her and Craig Stebic. She claimed that it was a platonic relationship, but that she had just gotten too casual, accepting his invitation to bring her family over and swim in their pool and join him for a cook-out. Jacobson ended up off the air, and her marriage ended, as well. Jacobson negotiated with NBC to leave her job and even filed a multi-million dollar lawsuit against the CBS station for airing the footage.

For a time, the scandal put the Lisa Stebic story back on the front page and into the forefront of everyone's mind. Then, like all news stories, it eventually faded from public memory and scrutiny. Although the family of Lisa Stebic maintains their reward and a website dedicated to finding her, and the Plainfield police still consider the case open, with each passing year, the case grows more and more cold. Craig Stebic continues to live in Plainfield and has, so far, continued to refuse to take a lie detector test or do anything that might help the police find his wife. Before too long, the story of Drew Peterson became the dominant story, with its eerie similarities to the Stebic case.

As for Amy Jacobson, she vanished from television for a while. She appeared on a number of radio shows for a time. She also did news and traffic on WLS radio. She is now a co-host of her own radio show on a local Chicago AM radio station. The Jacobson part of the story was later fictionalized and became part of an episode of *Law & Order*.

Lisa Stebic remains missing, and with the lead suspect unwilling to help, police have been frustrated. They have found no further evidence of what might have happened to her. There has been no evidence of foul play. There has been no DNA evidence, or any remnant of the brown-haired, brown-eyed mother of two.

Lisa Stebic's family continues to do what they can to keep her story alive. Lisa's story has appeared on national news programs such as *Nancy Grace's* program on HLN. Videos of Lisa have been posted on YouTube. Lisa's case has also been taken over by the Major Crimes Task Force for Grundy County, where she lived and disappeared, but nothing much has happened since that was announced in 2010.

Chapter Six
Helen Brach

If you have ever walked into a store and bought some candy, more than likely you have seen the Brach name. They are famous for their collections of hard candy, which used to be for sale by the pound in grocery stores around the country. At one time, a person could walk into the store and up to the loose candy and fill plastic bags with their own assortment. These days, the Brach candy is often pre-packaged at the plant. However, their assortment has remained an all-American staple and satisfied many a sweet-tooth across the country and around the world. All of that started in the Chicago area.

That's the side of the Brach name and product that most people remember. Many people fondly remember visiting those grocery stores and sneaking a piece of candy. Or, they remember their mothers and grandmothers loading up on caramels or butterscotch candies to hand out to the children later in the day. However, the Brach family, at least throughout the Chicago area, is also known for something far more sinister. It centers around the candy-fortune heiress Helen Brach, and is one of the most enduring mysteries in the area.

Although people were eventually brought to trial and even convicted for her disappearance, those involved claim that they do not know where she ended up, and that is part of the ongoing mystery. What exactly did happen to Helen Brach and where is her body? The theories abound, but they remain only that, theories.

Helen Brach, as you might imagine, lived a life of relative luxury. She married the man who was the heir to the Brach candy fortune and settled into her life of big houses and lots of land and had little interest in how candy was made. She was very much in love with her husband, and by all accounts, she was devastated when he passed away. Helen Brach was a quiet person, and she was content to live in her mansion in the northern suburbs of Chicago and indulge in her true passions. She loved animals, and she had a number of them within her house. Although she loved dogs and cats, her true love was always horses and she owned several throughout her lifetime. Unfortunately, this also brought her into contact with some of the most notorious, and notoriously evil, people who have ever existed in and around the Chicago area.

Chicago has several racetracks in and around the city. That means there is gambling and lots of money involved, and that always attracts people who are less than desirable. This is not only true when the horses are race horses, but also when the horses are show horses. Horses cost a lot to maintain and a good horse can bring a fortune to the breeders and those who buy and sell them. This was the life that Helen Brach somehow managed to find herself in as she entered her older years.

Helen Brach has lived a very normal life for most of her existence. Then, as she was getting on in years, she came into contact with a man named Richard Bailey. Richard Bailey was a charming person, who just happened to be a con man. He also happened to be a man who was schooled in the art of the con game from one of the most notorious villains that Chicago had ever seen: Silas Jayne.

Silas Jayne was a man who was no stranger to criminality. He started his life of violence at the age of 8 when he was bitten by a goose on his parent's farm. While most kids his age would have run screaming and crying to their home, Silas took a slightly different plan of attack. He calmly walked back to his home, grabbed an axe, and then proceeded to hack and chop and destroy every single goose in the flock. He came home, proud of himself, hours later covered in blood and goose feathers, leaving behind a field and pond filled with bloody carnage. This would prove to be a first step in his years of violence and criminal behavior.

At the age of 17, Silas Jayne committed the first act that would put him in jail. He pulled his car up next to a young woman and invited her to head into town to get a soda. Instead, he pulled into a quiet area and raped her. His stepfather, a lawyer, decided that jail time was what Silas needed to be scared straight and he agreed to give Silas a year in prison. If he hoped that Silas would learn something, he was very wrong, and the young man who emerged from prison was angrier, more violent, and more determined to cause as much chaos as he could.

The saga of Silas Jayne is long and sordid. He may have been responsible for several murders. He ultimately went to jail for soliciting a hitman to kill his half-brother, George, in the man's own basement while he was celebrating a birthday with his family. Anytime anyone tried to step in front of Silas Jayne to stop him and his plans, he would do everything he could to get his way. This included murder, or terrorist-like activities, even explosives and bombs.

What really made Silas his money was his horse business. Even though he was a cold-eyes murderer, he also had a talent for finding horse flesh. He made millions by buying and selling horses and by training horses for horse shows all over the Midwest and other parts of the country. He ran stables where other horse owners housed their

animals. Finally, he offered horse riding lessons for young men and women in and around the Chicago area.

Silas Jayne was also a con man. He would buy and sell horses that were useless. One of his favorite tactics was getting a young teenage girl interested in horseriding and offer lessons. He would then blackmail their fathers into buying horses for the young girls. He would often claim that the young girl had been engaging in sexual activities with stable hands and threatened to leak the information, destroying the girl's reputation. Many a father ended up with horses worth far less than what Silas was asking for through this method.

It was into this world that Richard Bailey came. Although Silas was in the midst of his trial for the murder of his half-brother when Bailey and Helen Brach met, there are many who feel that Silas offered advice and helped orchestrate the con that was pulled on Brach. With her inherited money and desire to help out horses, she must have seemed like the perfect target.

Richard Bailey was not a nice man. He had a specific target in mind for his con jobs. He looked for lonely, rich, elderly women. He would then swoop in and wine and dine them, showering them with praise and affection. In return, many of these women, desperate for affection from anyone as young as Bailey, showered him with gifts and money. Then, when he grew bored, or it seemed like the woman had caught on to the con, or he felt that the money might run out, he would leave them. He'd left a string of broken hearts, empty bank accounts, and miserable, sad women behind him, even before he met Helen Brach.

By the time Bailey met Brach he was running his own stables, known as the Bailey Stables. He looked like a wealthy man, filled with charm, and he had a way of wooing older women. According to stories Helen told her friends, he came in and swept her off her feet, which was not something she'd had happen in her life for a very long time. Bailey met Brach in 1973.

One of Bailey's most famous scams was to insinuate himself into the life of a wealthy socialite woman. At some point, he would come to her and say that he had found a particularly good horse that he wanted to invest in. However, his money was tied up in other investments and he needed a loan. Once the loan had been secured, he would not repay the loan. When Bailey then defaulted, the care of the animal fell to the woman he had been swindling. Often he would have set up the scam with co-conspirators, such as those who ran the stables, so that they would make some extra money once the loan had been defaulted.

Helen told friends that she was in love. Reportedly, Brach and Bailey were seen all about town. He wined and dined her and dazzled her, feeding into her desire for companionship, the way he had done many times before with other women. Many of Helen's friends were not so sure about this smooth-talking man, but Helen seemed happy for a few years. In return for his companionship, she provided gifts and lavished her attention upon him. Things continued through New Years Eve 1976 where Helen and Richard Bailey were seen out on the town and supposedly "danced the night away."

Prior to their partying the night away to celebrate the new year, in 1975, Bailey's brother had approached Helen saying that he had found some horses that she should invest in. He sold her three horses for a total price of $98,000. Helen did not know that her lover, Richard, was also involved in the sale and looking to profit from the deal. What Brach did not know, too, was that the horses were worth much, much less. In fact, the horses she purchased were worth less than $20,000. Brach was also told to invest in a couple of expensive brood mares at the same time.

As 1976 wore on, Brach became suspicious of Bailey and their relationship began to sour. Then, in 1977, Bailey and another co-conspirator put together a huge show of horses for Brach. They were trying to convince her to invest $150,000 in several of them. Brach attended the showing and then left after only an hour. She felt that she was being swindled by Bailey and his deceptions were beginning to show.

Brach hired an appraiser to come view the animals she had previously purchased from Bailey's brother. The appraiser told her that the three horses she had invested in were nearly worthless and that she should not sink a single dime into trying to train them. Prior to this, Bailey had been trying to convince her to invest $50,000 in training the three horses. Brach then visited the expensive brood mares she had purchased and also felt that they were worth just a fraction of what Bailey had told her they were worth.

Helen was, according to friends, a "phone addict." She would spend hours and hours talking on the phone to friends and family. She had an entire house almost to herself, except for when she was entertaining Bailey or with her handyman Jack Matnick. When she decided that Bailey was a crook, she told a friend of her's via telephone that she thought so. Her friend, it turned out, was also a friend with a state prosecutor. That friend told Brach that if she had any information about what Bailey was up to, she should give the information to the state prosecutor and the state could bring charges against Bailey.

Helen had an upcoming appointment at one of the most prestigious and renowned medical facilities in the world: The Mayo Clinic, located in Minnesota. She told her friend that she would be glad to visit the State's Attorney's office when she returned and that she had information that would likely send Richard Bailey to prison. In February of 1977, Helen Brach boarded a plane for Minnesota and visited her doctors at the Mayo Clinic. She never returned.

Her doctors confirmed that she showed up for her appointment. She was seen by several people afterwards, as well, as she bustled around in the frozen Minnesota winter. She even stopped into a gift shop and picked up a few items, saying that she was in a hurry because her "houseman was waiting." Did she mean Matnick? Where was he waiting? He was allegedly back in Chicago and she was still in Minneapolis.

Matnick, meanwhile, was casting suspicion on himself. He did not report to anyone that Brach had not arrived when she said she was supposed to. Instead, he purchased a meat grinder for the kitchen and had a room re-carpeted and repainted. He told police that Brach had arrived on a certain flight and gave them the flight information. The problem was that the air crew did not recall seeing her on the plane. No one seemed to know what had happened to Brach. Matnick stated that she had expressed a desire to go off alone, but her friends said that she would never do that and then not call. She always called and for four days, she had not called a soul.

Matnick then also cashed several checks that were reportedly signed by Brach. Finally, one of Helen's relatives showed up at her house. They found Matnick there alone and he gave them a bunch of stories that did not add up. The alarm was finally raised and police were called.

At first, the investigation focused on Matnick. What was this meat grinder? Had he killed her and then ground her up? Police inspected the tool and found that it was much too small and under-powered to be of any use in grinding up a human. And Matnick simply claimed that the room he repainted and re-carpeted had been one of his tasks as a handyman. He also claimed it was common for Brach to let him cash checks when he needed money to make repairs.

Police were still suspicious and Matnick was forced to repay some of the money he cashed with the checks. He insisted that he felt Helen Brach was still alive, but had gone off somewhere. He lived in Helen Brach's mansion for some time before finally moving out and retiring into obscurity. Prosecutors felt that they never had enough evidence against Matnick to make charges stick and they certainly felt they did not have enough to convict him in court.

Once Matnick was disposed of as a less-than-viable suspect, suspicion turned toward Richard Bailey. As the police began to investigate, they found that Bailey had cheated numerous other women and they soon found out who some of his associates were. When they saw that he knew and hung around with Silas Jayne, the alarm bells went off.

Bailey, as you might expect, claimed he did not know anything about what happened to Helen. He also denied that he had defrauded the heiress. Police, however, were able to find enough evidence to bring charges against the con man. Although the police believed that Bailey had conspired with several other men to hire someone to kill Brach and then dispose of her body, they had no certain evidence of it, so they arrested him and tried him for defrauding her of thousands of dollars.

The trial captivated the city of Chicago. Everyone was hoping that, at some point, Bailey would break and tell the world what he had actually done to Helen Brach. There were a lot of rumors, and there continue to be, but Bailey has never admitted anything and never revealed where Brach might be located.

Bailey was convicted. The judge made it clear that Bailey was not convicted of conspiracy to murder Brach, but he went on record saying that he believed that was exactly what Bailey had done. Bailey appealed his sentence, but that appeal was denied. Bailey also appealed for a new trial, saying new evidence had been found that had not previously been present when he was first convicted. That was also denied.

Helen Brach was finally declared dead in 1984. Her fortune was divided up among her brothers and sisters and other relatives. Richard Bailey got nothing out of it. Since Bailey's conviction, there have been those who have worked with both Bailey and Silas Jayne who have come forward and claimed they know what happened.

One associate claimed that he had been involved in several scams with both Jayne and Bailey and had been trying to get out of the business. Apparently, this angered Silas Jayne, already cooling in prison for conspiring to commit murder against his own brother, and he decided that something needed to be done with Brach. This associate claimed that several known Jayne associates arrived at his home late one night, claiming they needed help with something.

The story goes that this former associate was taken outside and the trunk of a car was opened. Inside was a carpet that was tightly wrapped around something. He claimed that he also saw the carpet move and that he heard groaning. One of the men there put a gun in his hand and told him to fire into the carpet, or he would be the one dead and put into the trunk. He claimed that he fired the gun and then got into the car. According to this story, Helen Brach was driven to the steel mills that were still operating at that time in Northwest Indiana and her body, along with the carpet, was thrown into the intense fire.

No evidence of this has ever been found. No trace of Helen Brach's body has ever been found. No one has come forward to confess to the crime, and the story about the body in the carpet could not be verified

by anyone. Even the confessor stated he had no idea, with any certainty, who was wrapped up inside that carpet.

Silas Jayne got out of prison for conspiring to murder his brother. He continued to protest his innocence, always claiming he was put into prison because he had knowledge that would have destroyed Illinois Governor Jim Thompson. He protested his innocence until he died, in the early '80s, of cancer.

Silas' family continues to be involved in crimes. He did not have children of his own, but he had nieces and nephews. Several of Silas Jayne's nephews have been involved in scams, such as burning down property to try and collect insurance on it. His legacy continues as one of the most notorious criminals the city has ever seen, despite being less well known than criminals like Al Capone, John Wayne Gacy, or Richard Speck.

Chapter Seven
Three Girls at the Indiana Dunes

The Indiana Dunes in the Chicago area are close to what The Hamptons are for New Yorkers. Although it is not quite the place where wealthy Chicagoans go to spend the summer, it is the place where harried Chicagoans will go in order to get away from the hustle and bustle of the city for a weekend or a day. It is an area at the southern tip of Lake Michigan, just far enough away from the city of Chicago to feel like a vacation spot, and close enough that most Chicagoans can spend the day there and get home in time for dinner. It is filled with sandy beaches, boating, and small resort towns that make most of their income during the summer months as city dwellers flock to the beaches to cool off and catch some rays.

It has been this way for a long time. Many a Chicagoan spent their prom weekends getting away to the Indiana Dunes. Many Chicagoans who own boats spend time in the waters off of the Dunes. There are towns in northwest Indiana, such as Chesterton, who rely almost entirely on the tourist dollars that come in during those summer months.

Normally, the Dunes are a quiet place. Yes, the area gets filled with tourists and beach-goers, but most people feel safe there. It is generally a family place, where parents can spend a day at the beach and not worry about what their kids are up to for a while. However, during the 1960s, the Indiana Dunes may have been the site of one of the most enduring mysteries in the city's history.

Renee Bruhl was a 19-year-old girl in 1966. She had just gotten married. The pressures of being a young bride were taking their toll on her and her marriage. However, on July 2, 1966, she was just one of hundreds of people who wanted to get away from the Chicago area and spend some time at the Indiana Dunes. She planned to spend the entire day with her two friends Patricia Blough and Ann Miller.

All three women were fond of horses. In fact, this brought them in contact with the now-infamous Silas Jayne. Blough and Miller reportedly had horses they were boarding at a stable owned by the man. It was thought that both women enjoyed going to the stables on weekends and riding the horses and all three seemingly had some skill.

That morning it was Miller who decided to drive. The two girlfriends knew that Bruhl was not happy in her marriage. She complained that her husband of fifteen months preferred to spend all of his free time with friends and tuning up hot rods to spending time with her. She was wondering if she should get out of the relationship now. The day at the beach was meant as a way to cheer up Bruhl, have a great girls' day out, and forget about their troubles.

Miller had the largest car. They then drove the long journey from the Chicago suburbs into northwest Indiana and then to the Indiana Dunes. Miller parked the car in the standard parking lot at 10 a.m. that day and the girls were later seen on the beach, lying on beach towels in their swimsuits soaking up the sun. According to witnesses, the girls were lying on their towels about 100 yards from the shoreline.

Around noon, the three women were seen leaving their beach towels and heading into the water. Above them, the sun was high and hot. The day was hot and beautiful, with few clouds. While they were in the water, witnesses would say they saw the three women speaking to a young man with a tan complexion who was also in the water operating a boat with a blue interior. The boat was described as being about fourteen to sixteen feet long and running with an outboard motor. This would be the last time anyone could be sure that the women were seen.

It was another couple who had reported that they'd seen the three young women enter the water and talking to the young man in the boat. They lost track of what was happening with the three women after that. When dusk came, the young couple gathered up their belongings and began to head back to their car, and it was then that they noticed that the belongings for the three young women they had seen earlier in the day were still sitting on the beach, unclaimed.

Eventually, more witnesses would come forward. Some said that they thought they saw the young women climb aboard the white boat with the blue interior and that the boat headed off in a western direction, up a small river nearby. Others were not sure, and some claimed to have seen the women walking down the boardwalk near the beach, eating ice cream and other food available there.

Bruhl left behind a large beach towel, her blouse, cigarettes, a pair of shorts, her suntan lotion, 25 cents, and her purse, which, upon being opened, was shown to contain $55 in uncashed checks. Miller and Blough had also left their belongings. They were collected by a park ranger and stored in their lost and found for days. In fact, it wasn't until after the July 4 holiday that anyone from the girl's family came forward and told the park rangers that their daughters were missing.

It was Blough's father who called the park ranger office. He told the park ranger superintendent that his daughter was missing and had been last seen at the Dunes. He also wondered if there were any traces of his daughter that had been left behind. It was then that the park rangers learned a missing persons report had been filed on all three women. The rangers began investigating.

They found the Buick still parked in the parking lot. There was no sign that it had been touched or that anyone had attempted to move it. The rangers soon called in the Coast Guard, in case the three women had been pulled out into the lake and drowned. They began combing the Dunes, hoping to find some trace of the women. The formal search began on July 5 and was soon expanded to include the Ogden Dunes, which adjoined the Dunes where the women had been seen, in case they had wandered over there. Again, they came up empty.

When investigators came and collected Bruhl's purse, they opened it and found the money and the checks. They also found a note she had written to her husband, Jeffrey, telling him that she was running out of patience with his running around with his friends and wanted to get out of the marriage. Jeffrey claimed that this was the first he had heard of this and had no idea that there was any concern or strife within the marriage. Bruhl's own family came forward and defended Jeffrey and agreed that their daughter probably wrote the note after a fight and had never intended to actually give it to her husband.

A hopeful clue was found when more witnesses came forward. Another tourist had been on the beach that day and he had been taking home movies with his eight millimeter movie camera. He offered the reels he had taken that day to investigators. Sure enough, they thought that they caught something.

They saw two boats in the background. Several other witnesses had come forward confirming that they had seen the three girls getting onto a boat driven by the young man with the tan complexion. Investigators thought they saw two boats on the reels of film that matched the description. One was a sixteen- to eighteen-foot trimaran fiberglass boat with a three-hull configuration. The second was a twenty-six- to twenty-eight-foot Trojan cabin cruiser. In the case of the smaller boat, investigators thought they could see three women matching the descriptions of the missing women sitting on the boat. However, on the larger boat they thought they could see three men and three other women sitting on the deck.

The larger boat was reportedly seen at about 3 p.m. It was thought that it might have been possible that the three girls got on the smaller boat, which then, in turn, took them to the larger boat. However, other witnesses claimed to have seen the three girls on the boardwalk eating

ice cream after 3 p.m. Some more witnesses claimed that as the girls walked along the beach, they were seen speaking to another man, not the young man with the tan skin, who may have also been on the cabin cruiser. Witnesses who saw the cruiser said that the boat appeared to have radios and an antenna, but that there was no name on the stern.

Did they swim out and drown? According to their families, that seemed unlikely. Blough was rated as an excellent swimmer, capable of swimming solidly for twenty or thirty miles. Miller was also thought to be an excellent swimmer, perhaps even a match for Blough. Bruhl might have been the weakest of them, but even her family felt that she should have been able to handle any situation they might have run into while in the water and make it back to shore.

As investigators looked deeper, they found the girls' love for horses. They found that Miller and Blough had boarded their horses at local stables, and this had put them into contact with known criminals in the horse-breeding world. In fact, there was a rumor that Blough had told friends she had been having problems with people she described as "horse syndicate people." What did that mean? No one knew for sure and no one at the stables the girls used was able to tell investigators anything.

The two women with horses frequently rode them at the Tri Color Stables, which were owned by Silas' brother, George Jayne. Silas would attempt, several times, to kill his half-brother. Once, Silas, or someone he hired, strapped dynamite to George's Cadillac. When George came out in the morning, with his champion rider, Cheryl Ann Rude, he handed her the keys and asked her if she could move the car while he opened the doors to the barn. Seconds after she turned the key, the car exploded. Rude was killed and George was shaken to his core.

Bruhl supposedly once told a friend that she had received a facial injury while at he stables. No one was sure when she said this, but it was thought that it was around June of 1965, the same time that George's exploding car killed the rider. Was it possible that Blough was there? Had debris from the explosion injured her? Had she been there earlier and seen something that would have pinned the crime on the perpetrator, or perhaps Silas Jayne?

Silas Jayne had nothing to say to investigators. Investigators, meanwhile, had no evidence to charge him with anything. One time, however, Silas was chatting with a policeman and stated that he "had three bodies buried" under his house. Before a warrant could be issued, the cop who had heard the statement died suddenly and the matter was forgotten. The case of the three women faded into history and more pressing matters involving Silas Jayne came to the fore.

In recent years, another theory has developed. At least two of the girls, it was rumored, might have been pregnant. Bruhl was having trouble with her marriage, and she didn't want to have a child. It was also thought that Miller might have been three months along. All three women, supposedly, were afraid to tell their parents of what was going on. It was 1966 and abortions were not yet legal in the United States, but there were abortionists who were running operations illegally.

One of the best ways to do that was to run them on boats. Purportedly, the abortionists would send runners to the beaches to meet up with the young women who were to have the operations. They would then transport them on smaller boats to larger boats that were anchored far away from the shore, away from prying eyes and people who might ask questions. One theory is that the three women knew that the Indiana Dunes was a place to meet a runner who could then take them to the boat on the lake to take care of their little problems.

Could it be that two of the women had babies that they didn't want? Were they taken out into the lake, aboard a larger cabin cruiser boat, to have that operation? Could it be that something went wrong with one of the operations and one of the girls ended up dead? Then, in a panic, and not wanting witnesses, were the other two killed and all three dumped into the cold, unforgiving waters of Lake Michigan?

One of the investigators who has relentlessly pursued this case for years, Dick Wylie, a crime reporter for several newspapers, thinks so. In fact, he thinks that a man named Ralph Largo, Jr., was the man responsible. Largo was known to run an illegal abortion operation out of his home in Gary, Indiana. It was known that Largo's aunt and uncle also performed illegal abortions out of their home in Gary.

To this day, there are only theories. Over the years, there have even been sightings of the three women. In each case, those tips were tracked down, but lead to nothing. There was also a psychic who claimed that she had a vision of the three women being buried beneath sand dunes and investigators headed back out to the sand and dug them up, but found nothing. However, over the years, with wind and rain, snow and floods, and the ever-flowing current of the lake itself, the Dunes are constantly changing shape. The Dunes now, look nothing like they did the day the three women vanished.

It was as if the three women just simply ceased to exist. Their families have never had remains to bury, and their disappearance continues to be a mystery. Whatever the theories, it seems as if the three women met with a bad ending. They were either killed and buried beneath the house of a horse-breeder who was also a monster, or they were murdered and dumped into the water because of a botched abortion.

No one has ever been brought to justice for the disappearance. Their killer, for all anyone knows, may still be at large.

Part Three
Murder and Mayhem

No collection of unsolved mysteries in Chicago would be complete without a look at the darkest side of the city. Chicago has been a city connected with murder for a long time, going back to the days of Fort Dearborn. It was the heart of gangster history during the 1930s. It was the main headquarters for the busiest office that the FBI had going at the time. It was the place where John Dillinger met his end via a bullet at the hands of Melvin Purvis and his G-men. To say that the streets of Chicago have run red with blood is not entirely an exaggeration.

The police force of Chicago is relentless in their pursuit of these criminals. The sheer number of crimes that do get solved within the Windy City is staggering. Most of the crimes, however, are small, and not the kind that end up in the news or with everyone in the world talking about them.

Still, there are some very famous crimes that have yet to be solved. This is not for lack of trying on the part of investigators; it just means that the right clue has yet to be discovered that will lead investigators to the right person, so that a formal charge can be made. In some cases, these crimes gained worldwide attention and changed things for everyone. In some cases, only the families involved remain to wonder who committed the atrocity against their loved ones.

Chapter Eight
The Tylenol Murders

Imagine, if you will, having a headache. It's the kind of headache that makes focusing on work or your life almost impossible. Fortunately, in your collection of medicines, you probably have the cure. More than likely, even now, there is a bottle of aspirin, Excedrin, or Tylenol sitting in your medicine cabinet. So, with your head pounding and your hands shaking, you walk into the bathroom, open the medicine cabinet, and grab the bottle, shake a few pills in your hand, and then down them with a sip of water. Hopefully, you think, my headache will be gone in a few minutes. However, what if that pill you took was laced with cyanide and, instead, you ended up collapsing on the floor, unable to breathe.

In 1982, this nightmare actually happened in and around the Chicago area. It was a crime so shocking that it shook the entire world and changed the way products, and medication in particular, were packaged. To this day, despite repeated attempts to re-open the case by the FBI, no one has ever been caught, tried, or convicted of the Tylenol murders.

It all started September 29, 1982, in the western suburb of Elk Grove Village. Twelve-year-old Mary Kellerman awoke that morning feeling like she had a fever and a sore throat. She walked into her parent's room and complained of the sore throat. Her mother got up and got her some Extra Strength Tylenol, gave her one tablet, and sent her back to bed. Her mother went back to bed as well. Hours later, Mary's mother awoke and went to check on Mary. She was not in her room. As she continued to look for her daughter, she eventually checked the bathroom. Mary was on the floor, unresponsive. Her frantic mother called the paramedics and she was rushed to the hospital. At first, it was thought the young girl had actually suffered from a stroke. She was pronounced dead at the hospital. However, as investigators looked further, they were eventually able to find there was a far more sinister reason for this child's death.

That same day, in another Chicago suburb, Arlington Heights, a man named Adam Janus also had a headache. He reached into his medicine cabinet and grabbed his bottle of Extra Strength Tylenol and popped a couple of the capsules. Hours later, he was found unresponsive, and was rushed to the hospital. He, too, died and, initially, it was thought that he had a massive heart attack. At that moment, no connection between the two cases was made and no one could imagine the evil that had been unleashed on the unsuspecting public.

The tragedy got even worse when Adam Janus' family got together to mourn the loss of their brother and friend and to make funeral plans. His brother, Stanley, and his wife Theresa, both had headaches. The stress was too much for them. As the family gathered in Adam's living room, Stanley went searching for something for the headache. He found Adam's bottle of Extra Strength Tylenol. He gave a capsule to his wife, Theresa, and then took one of his own. As the shocked family looked on, Stanley, and then Theresa, both collapsed. The paramedics were called back to the house and both were taken. Stanley died that night, having never regained consciousness. Theresa died a few days later.

Investigators were puzzled. Was it something in the house? They began searching everything in Adam's home. Since Adam's incident had taken place in a different suburb than Mary Kellerman's, the investigators in both areas did not discuss similarities. There was more death on its way.

Mary McFarland, also of a western suburb, this time Elmhurst, was the next to fall. She, too, took Extra Strength Tylenol for a headache and was soon added to the list of victims.

Just days later, Mary Reiner of Winfield, who was home from the hospital recovering from the birth of her son, fell.

The very same day that Mary Reiner fell, an airline stewardess from Chicago-based United Airlines, Paula Prince, was found dead in her suburban home

Now investigators were starting to talk. Something very strange was going on as perfectly healthy men and women were dropping dead all over the suburbs, seemingly, for no reason at all.

One investigator started looking for other incidents and came across the Janus case. He contacted the investigators on that case and they began to compare the incident of Mary Kellerman and then noticed other cases. The one thing that each had in common was a bottle of Extra Strength Tylenol near the crime scene. Each had consumed a capsule before collapsing and then dying. Something was wrong with the bottles of pain reliever, but the question was: Was it an accident that happened at the factory or had someone done the unthinkable? Had someone tampered with bottles of Tylenol around the city in a deliberate attempt to kill people? The implications sent shivers down the spines of investigators and they immediately issued a warning.

Police began driving up and down the streets of the Chicago suburbs broadcasting alerts that the Tylenol in their cabinets might have been tampered with or dangerous. For Johnson & Johnsons, the owners of Tylenol, it was a devastating blow. It was going to cost them billions to recall all of the capsules on store shelves and try to find out what had happened. In a precedent-setting move they went to the public and said that they would do anything and everything to make sure that their customers were safe. They released the apparent lot numbers of the pills that appeared to have been tampered with. They assured the public that steps would be taken to prevent anything like it from happening again.

The company also pulled the capsules from store shelves. They sent alerts to hospitals asking them to stop prescribing or using Tylenol. They also halted production of Tylenol, shutting down the production lines completely. It was thought that, at the time, there were over 30 million bottles of pills in circulation at that time. It was estimated that the total value of those pills was somewhere around $100 million.

Panic hit the city, and then spread across the country like wildfire. The national news soon picked up on the story and Johnson & Johnson took out ads in nationally read publications. People became paranoid about taking any medications. The revenue of many of the leading pharmaceutical manufacturers suffered. Investigators, meanwhile, were trying to pool their resources to figure out what happened.

It seemed as if someone had taken the Tylenol Extra Strength tablets from the shelves and then removed the plastic tops and cotton, injected several capsules with cyanide and then closed up the bottles, put them back in the boxes and put the boxes back on store shelves. At the time, doing this was incredibly easy as there were no tamper-resistant bottles. The flaws in the system were shockingly exposed.

It was discovered that only the capsules had been tampered with. Thus, the tablets that had been produced by Tylenol were fine. This did little to stem the panic, however, as people were afraid to take anything with the Tylenol name on it. The problem was that the crime itself was virtually undetectable. This was not a time when every store had dozens of cameras that taped the movements of every customer. It was entirely possible for a criminal to tamper with products, place them on shelves, and for no one to be the wiser.

One thing was in the favor of investigators. The pills that had been tampered with looked different from the pills that were not tampered with. They tended to bulge strangely and be slightly deformed from the tampering. To the casual user, however, there was little difference.

The panic began to spread beyond just worries about Tylenol. Hospitals across the country were flooded with phone calls and panicked people in their ERs worried that they had been poisoned. There were so many calls to the Seattle Poison Control Center that they issued a statement to the public stating that if they had been poisoned with cyanide, they would likely be dead long before they could have called the poison control or sought medical help.

The makers of Tylenol, meanwhile, had spent considerable amounts of money tearing apart their factory. They were soon able to determine that the cyanide had not been introduced into the product at the factory. With that, the DEA, FBI, and other national investigating agencies pooled together to try and find the culprit. They had a daunting task ahead of them.

The first thing investigators did was to take a look at the bottles of pills that had already been pulled from shelves. They soon found other bottles that had been tampered with and pills laced with cyanide. They also found six Chicago suburban stores where there were tampered bottles. A Jewel Food store in Arlington Heights, Jewel Foods in Grove Village, Osco Drugs in Schaumburg, Walgreens in Chicago, Frank's Finer Foods in Winfield, and another store that was not disclosed. In each case, they found up to ten bottles in each store that had been tampered with. The one exception was an Osco Drug where just two bottles were found.

It appeared to investigators that the tampering had been entirely at random. At the same time, national security forces were worried that a terrorist organization might have been at work and had deliberately targeted certain stores. Another theory was that the person held a personal grudge against Tylenol and Johnson & Johnson. The same person might have also been in a personal war against the stores he had placed the bottles; at the same time there was another theory that the person involved just held a grudge against society in general. It was a wide pool of potential suspects with that range.

The FBI came in and began using their relatively new profiling techniques. Poison was predominantly a murder weapon used by women. However, they felt that a man was the most likely culprit in this case. The reasons for the attack were wide and varied. With the possible profile in place, and just a month after the attacks began, the police had their first suspect in custody.

Police brought in a 48-year-old suspect who was an amateur chemist. He was also a dockhand who worked a distribution center for Tylenol products. The distribution center supplied bottles to several of the stores where tampered bottles had been found. Investigators stated, when they questioned the suspect, that he had previously worked on a chemistry product that used cyanide. Investigators also searched his apartment and found two one-way tickets to Thailand and a strange book that, according to investigators, contained detailed methods for putting poison into capsules.

The police thought that they had their man. They had one problem: they had no real hard evidence to arrest the dockhand and charge him with the crime. Yes, he possessed some illegal items, such as firearms, but they had no absolute proof that he had walked into stores, purchased

Tylenol bottles, poisoned them and then returned them to shelves. They sent him to jail for firearms possession and he ended up being released on a $6,000 bond. In the meantime, something else had developed that put someone else entirely on their list.

Johnson & Johnson received a letter, claiming to be from the culprit. Police were familiar with this kind of thing. If it was a terrorist act, this would be when the terrorist would ask for demands. If this was a maniac, it would have ramifications and echoes to other famous cases such as the Zodiac Killer from San Francisco, who sent taunting letters to police and local newspapers. The letter taunted the huge drug company, bragging about how easy it was to tamper with their products and bring about terror to the masses. It then demanded $1 million to stop the tampering. The person who wrote the letter demanded that the company respond in the pages of the *Chicago Tribune.*

Johnson & Johnson decided it was worth the gamble to ignore the taunts and the threats and they went to authorities. Eventually, they were able to trace the letter back to a man named James W. Lewis. Lewis was not unknown to authorities, especially in some parts of the country. Technically, his profession was that of an accountant. In reality, however, he was better known to law enforcement as a con man. He was also wanted for a brutal murder involving an elderly woman in Kansas City and he was also a suspect in a jewel robbery. When his name was identified as the source of the letter, an arrest warrant was issued for Lewis.

Chicago police and the FBI were now in a full manhunt for Lewis. While they were searching, however, another tainted bottle of Tylenol capsules was found on the north side of Chicago, in a drug store not far from where Paula Prince had purchased her fatal tainted bottle. Authorities immediately took the bottle and dusted it for fingerprints or other evidence. They came up empty.

The FBI and police were sending out images of Lewis to every news agency across the country. They followed up leads throughout Illinois, as well as Missouri, Kansas, and Texas. They handed out photos of Lewis and they produced descriptions of him and any of his known colleagues. They also wanted to talk to Lewis' wife, LeAnn.

Just after the new bottle of pills was found, a letter arrived at the *Chicago Tribune* offices from a man calling himself Robert Richardson. In the letter, Richardson said that neither himself nor his wife had anything to do with the Tylenol murders and that he and his wife were unarmed. When the *Tribune* and authorities probed further, they discovered that Robert Richardson was one of several aliases used by James W. Lewis. The letter was postmarked from New York.

The FBI immediately activated their agents in the New York area to start scouring their contacts and the city for information on where Lewis might have been. While this was happening, Johnson & Johnson stated on November 11, 1982 that they would be re-introducing their products to store shelves. They had completely redesigned the packaging, making them tamper-resistant and making it so any bottles that had been tampered with would be easier to spot. No one knew if customers would return to buying the pain relievers and many in the business world held their breath. To their surprise, it took less than two months for consumer confidence to be totally restored and Tylenol began to be bought by the public at rates that equalled those before the tampering incidents.

While that was happening, the FBI got their biggest lead in tracking down Lewis. They heard from a librarian from the New York Public Library who claimed to have seen Lewis several times at the library. The librarian had seen the wanted posters that were posted at the library and was certain the man in the poster was the man seen at the library. The FBI moved in and hope was high that the culprit who had so brutally murdered seven people in Chicago would be caught.

On December 13, 1982, FBI agents swarmed into the New York Public Library and surrounded James W. Lewis as he sat in the reading room. Not long after, his wife, LeAnn, was also arrested. Both of them were brought in for questioning.

Under the questioning, Lewis and his wife denied having anything to do with the Tylenol poisonings. In fact, Lewis denied having written the extortion letter, despite the fact his handwriting and the handwriting on the letter were an exact match.

Not long after his arrest, a second extortion letter was found. This one had been sent to the White House. In it, the letter writer had handwritten a note stating that a bomb would be set off and more Tylenol murders would occur unless President Ronald Reagan changed his tax policies. Lewis denied writing this, despite the handwriting matching that letter and his own handwriting yet again.

Although he had seemed like a good suspect at first, the FBI had nothing that they could pin on Lewis or his wife to show that they had anything to do with the poisonings. Plus, they were able to track evidence that showed the couple were living in a hotel in New York at the time of the Tylenol killings. They also proved that his wife, LeAnn, had been at her job every day during the time of the poisonings and her husband was seen joining her for lunch every day while she worked there.

The FBI and authorities looked for more leads. However, they could not find any bus, plane, or train tickets that showed they had left New York during that time to head to Chicago at any point during the killings.

69

It seemed as if the couple had to be ruled out and the evidence just was not lining up in the favor of investigators.

This was not a free and clear pass for Lewis, however. He was ultimately arrested and charged with extortion and six counts of mail fraud. He was found guilty and sentenced to twenty years in prison. He ended up serving thirteen of those years and was released in 1995.

As the days, weeks, and months went on, it became harder and harder for the FBI or police to find new leads. It was becoming obvious that things were not going to go as they had hoped. The FBI was trying to find new suspects, but they had nothing else to go on. So, they turned to their relatively new area and asked for a profile of the Tylenol killer from their profile experts.

After putting their heads together, the profilers came up with their profile. They said that the Tylenol killer was probably a loner and was likely very angry, either with himself, or society, or both. The profilers advised that investigators look for someone who had sought psychiatric treatment, perhaps even recently. The person might have reached out for help in dealing with extreme feelings, such as rage, depression, anxiety, or issues with control. They also felt this person was likely to have bragged to friends or associates about the killings in an attempt to get credit for them. They would have been likely to rage about the injustices in society and why they felt society might have done them wrong. It was thought that the killer likely lived in and around the Chicago area, would have owned a car or truck, and may have once worked in a profession that familiarized him with working with cyanide. This could mean that the killer worked with the gold or silver mining industry, film processing, or chemical manufacturing. Also, if he did work in any of those industries, the job he had was probably menial.

Even at the time, the profilers were criticized for being too broad in this description. It was thought that the profile was too general, and could apply to too many people and, therefore, was of little use to investigators. Despite this, the FBI has stated that the profile gave them some insight into the thinking habits and desires of the killer, if it did not provide them with an immediate suspect.

Eventually, the trail grew cold. There were no new bottles found and the industry had made changes to their packaging. It was now very difficult to get into a product in order to try tampering with them. However, a strange phenomenon did occur that had police departments across the country pulling out their hair and the FBI scrambling to find out if a network of terrorists was at work in the country. It also cost other companies, some nearly as big as Johnson & Johnson, millions of dollars as they had to deal with copycats.

In fact, incidents of product tampering rose that year. According to some studies, there were 270 suspected incidents of product tampering. Of those, once investigators searched the products, about 36 were proven to be real incidents of product tampering where someone was trying to do harm or cause death to others.

In Minneapolis, a young boy named Marlon Barrow came home from school and opened the fridge to take a drink of chocolate milk. Soon after he became violently sick and was taken to the hospital and treated. It was found that his milk had been tampered with and laced with poison.

In Florida, a 27-year-old man named Harry Browning simply went into his fridge and pulled out some orange juice. He did not notice anything wrong with it as he drank it, but soon fell ill and was rushed to the hospital. The orange juice had been tainted with insecticide. In the case of Barrow and Browning, no one died, luckily, but that was not the case with all of the copycats.

In February of 1986 a woman named Diane Elsroth, 23, was visiting her boyfriend in New York City. She had a headache and took a bottle of Tylenol and popped a capsule. It was one of the new tamper-proof bottles, so she felt confident about doing that. In minutes she suddenly fell ill and collapsed. She died at the hospital and it was found that she had ingested cyanide. When investigators went to her boyfriend's home they found that the bottle had three more tainted capsules still waiting inside.

Immediately, an alert went out and Tylenol bottles were recalled from local stores. To the horror of investigators, they found more bottles on store shelves containing cyanide-laced capsules. What was particularly worrying was that the culprit was able to tamper with the capsules and then repackage the bottles to make them look as if they had not been tampered with. Police and Johnson & Johnson thought that they were going to have to issue another huge recall. Then, no other tainted bottles were found and no one else died. Investigators were unable to find the culprit, but breathed a hesitant sigh of relief.

In June of 1986, another incident that reminded investigators of the Tylenol murders happened in the American northwest. In Washington state, a 40-year-old woman named Sue Snow was having a huge headache and looking for relief. She picked up her bottle of Excedrin and took a couple of capsules. Next, she went into her 15-year-old daughter's room to say good morning and then wandered into the bathroom to plug in her curling iron and take her shower. When her daughter became concerned over how long it was taking her mother, she opened the bathroom door. Her mother was on the floor, unresponsive. She called 911 and her mother was rushed to the hospital where doctors worked on her for a long time, trying to revive her. It was futile and Sue Snow died.

71

At first, doctors had no clue what had happened. Then, as an autopsy was performed, the medical examiner noticed the scent of bitter almonds wafting from the body. That is the tell-tale sign of cyanide poisoning. They took blood and tissue samples and confirmed that Sue Snow had died from cyanide poisoning. Bristol-Myers, the company that manufactured and packaged Excedrin, immediately issued a warning and then a national recall in hopes to avert anymore deaths.

The day after the national news was filled with the story that Bristol-Myers had recalled Excedrin, the police investigating Sue Snow's death got a call from a woman named Stella Nickell. She told police that, a few weeks before, her husband had died. Although the doctors had ruled his death natural causes, and likely a result of emphysema, she felt that he had died in a way similar to Sue Snow. She thought that he had been murdered by the same person who had poisoned the Excedrin pills. She claimed that he had collapsed and died shortly after taking Excedrin capsules.

Police were curious to see if this was the case. They immediately ran tests of her husband's blood. Sure enough, they found traces of cyanide. The police then found two bottles of Excedrin in Nickell's home that were tainted with poisoned capsules. It seemed that Nickell's husband had been the first death in what looked to be another serial killer's bizarre attack on the world. The police, however, as a matter of course, decided it was best to talk to Nickell. When that happened, some strange things started to emerge.

Police began to look through some of the bottles from the national recall. They found two more tainted bottles from the Washington area, not far from where Sue Snow and Stella Nickell lived. The tainted bottles were taken to Washington, D.C. to see if anything could be discovered about them. Under microscopic analysis, they found something strange. The bottles with tainted pills showed strange green specks on the pills inside. When they analyzed the specks, they discovered that the green specks were a product used by people with fish tanks to get rid of algae. In fact, the product was called Algae Destroyer.

Investigators went back to Nickell's home. They found that she had several fish tanks in her home. They also found that she routinely used Algae Destroyer on the tanks. In fact, she had recently purchased the Algae Destroyer at about the same time she had purchased the Excedrin bottles. Investigators felt that something was up.

They probed deeper, including talking to people in Nickell's family, such as her daughter. The first thing they found was that Nickell had taken out not one, but three life insurance policies on her husband before his death. The three policies were worth a combined total of $70,000.

When detectives began to probe a little further, they found that Nickell stood to gain an additional $100,000 from one of the insurance companies if she was able to prove to them that his death was accidental. They then spoke to the doctors who had treated her husband and found that Nickell had reacted angrily when they first diagnosed the reason for her husband's death as emphysema. That diagnosis would deny her that additional amount of money from the insurance company and she had stood in the ER arguing with medical personnel about their diagnosis rather than expressing any kind of upset or regret over her husband's death.

The FBI asked her to take a lie detector test. Nickell agreed and then promptly failed the test. Although that was not admissible as evidence, the investigators felt that Nickell had murdered her husband. Their theory is that she poisoned her husband and then spread other tainted bottles to make her husband's death seem random. Her purpose in doing this was two-fold, as she could try to cover up the murder by making it seem to be another in a series of random deaths and she could collect the insurance money by showing that his death was an accident and not anything to do with his health.

Two months later, the big break came. Investigators talked to Nickell's daughter. Her daughter was 27 and from a previous marriage and the two of them had a strained relationship. She revealed to investigators that Nickell had spoken to her in the past about how bored she was in the relationship with her husband. In fact, her daughter stated that her mother had confessed to her previously that she had tried to kill her husband using a poison called foxglove, but it had not succeeded. Her mother had confided in her that she had done some research into cyanide prior to her husband's death.

Investigators soon had enough evidence to charge Stella Nickell with the deaths of her husband and Sue Snow. Stella Nickell was put on trial for murder. In May of 1988, Stella Nickell was found guilty and sentenced to ninety years in prison. She will be eligible for parole in 2018.

Stella Nickell was the first person sent to prison for product tampering. She ended up not being the last. There were a rash of poisonings, most of the time with people trying to murder one specific person, often in their own family, but trying to make it look like a random event by a serial poisoner. As for the person who had committed the original crime and killed seven people in Chicago, the evidence was cold and investigators had no new leads. Johnson & Johnson had a $1,000 reward for information leading to the culprit and that remained unclaimed.

Over the years, there have been times when the case was opened and new suspects were investigated. Lewis was investigated again when it seemed that another spate of evidence was found, but it turned out not to lead to anything that might have led to a conviction. At one point, the FBI even investigated the man who would become famous as the Unabomber, Ted Kaczynski. He was in the Chicago area at the time and two of his earliest bombing efforts happened there. He also fit the profile of someone with a grudge against humanity. Although the FBI and investigators have yet to fully rule him out, they also have not found enough evidence as yet to bring additional charges against Kaczynski, who currently sits in a SuperMax prison for other crimes and murders.

To this day, the crimes remain unsolved. The ways in which products of all kinds are packaged were changed and made safer, for the most part, and incidents of product tampering have decreased over the years. The reward for information leading to the culprit still remains unclaimed, and the case still remains open in Chicago suburban police departments and within the FBI.

Chapter Nine
The Grimes Sisters

On December 28, 1956, two young girls, ages 13 and 15, vanished. For many in Chicago, this and another murder mystery from the 1950s is what caused Chicago to lose whatever might have remained of the city's innocence. On that particular date, with snow in the air and biting cold coming off Lake Michigan, the two young girls left home to do something that just about anyone and everyone else has done. They were going to see a movie. This was at a time when girls that young were allowed to head downtown to go to movies using public transportation and not be escorted. It was common. Although girls had vanished before this, it was just not thought possible that two girls who seemed so typical and who came from such a normal family could end up like the Grimes sisters did.

Barbara Grimes, 15, and her sister Patricia Grimes, 13, left their home in the evening on December 28, 1956. It was just days after Christmas and it was cold that night. The weather forecast called for snow in the next few days. The sisters were excited, however, because they were going to head down into the city to the Brighton Theater. Why were they so excited? Because the sisters were diehard Elvis Presley fans and Elvis' new movie *Love Me Tender* was out and playing at that theater.

The girls walked from their home that night and said good-bye to their parents. The movie was set to start after 9 p.m. Even taking the bus home, their parents expected them to be home before midnight. It was a Friday, so the girls were allowed to stay out later than had it been a school night. Their parents bid them farewell and went about their evening as normal, expecting the girls to come into the front door at about 11:45 p.m.

How they got to the theater is unknown. They both had about enough money to total about $2.15. They were dressed warmly on that cold night. They were spotted in line to buy some popcorn at the theater at 9:30 p.m. They were seen there by two friends. Of those friends, one would later tell authorities that the girls were standing in line, laughing and carrying on, but not in a strange way. They saw no one with them and the sisters appeared as if nothing was wrong or abnormal. Nothing seemed amiss at 9:30 p.m.

When their parents eventually called the police, at about 2:15 a.m., and word got out about the girls vanishing, more people came forward and offered information about where the girls might have been that night. For example, several witnesses would swear to police and testify that they saw the girls standing at the bus stop boarding the Archer bus headed east. That would take them back in the direction of their home. Witnesses said that the two girls got off at the Western Avenue stop, which was only about halfway to their home. As to why the girls would get off so early, no one could be sure. They were not seen meeting anyone and they were not seen with another person.

Back at their home, their parents got worried. Both of them had decided to stay up and wait for the girls to come home. When 11:45 came and went, they started to become more upset. When the 28th turned into the 29th, they really became worried. They hoped that the girls had met up with friends and lost track of time. Then 2:15 a.m. came and went and they called police.

Before long, the story of the Grimes sisters was all over the news in and around Chicago. Then, the word of their disappearance spread beyond the city. Word even got to their idol, Elvis Presley, who went on national television and pleaded with the girls to reach out to their parents or get back home. A massive search was conducted for the girls and their photos and images were plastered all over the city. When that happened, more people came forward with information, and strange things began to happen.

One man who came forward was a security guard who was on duty on the northwest side of the city on the night of the 28th. He said that he was certain that two girls matching the description of the sisters came to him on the morning of the 29th and asked him for directions. Where they went and what happened to them after that was unknown and it could never be absolutely established that the two girls he spoke to were the Grimes sisters.

Classmates of the two girls came forward and said that they were sure they had seen the girls on the 29th as well. They insisted that the two girls were in Angelo's Restaurant eating a meal that morning. The restaurant was located at 3551 South Archer Avenue. Whether or not this sighting was accurate was never determined.

At the same time, and on the same day, a railroad conductor insisted that he saw the two girls on a train on the far north side of the city. In fact, he insisted that he saw the two girls on a train that was in Glenview, which is an area well north of where they lived and of downtown Chicago. Again, whether or not this siting was valid is unknown.

A man who owned a restaurant located on West Madison said he saw the sisters near the D&L Restaurant. He said that he thought one of

the sisters, perhaps Patricia, was behaving as if she were drunk or very sick. He would also claim that they were being accompanied by a man who would later become a suspect named Edward L. "Benny" Bedwell. Once again, however, no one else could corroborate this claim.

On January 1, 1957, weeks after they'd disappeared, someone came forward saying he was sure he had seen the girls on a CTA bus. This time he claimed they were on a bus driving down Damen Avenue. Why they would have been there and why they could not have contacted their parents, especially with the news of their disappearance everywhere and their own faces staring out of the front page of every newspaper, is unknown.

Then, a report came on January 2, 1957, that a desk clerk at a downtown hotel claimed to have seen the girls. He reported to police that two girls that he believed matched the photos and description of the Grimes sisters had walked into the hotel and asked for a room. Since they were underage, he had turned them away, but did not know where they had gone from there.

On January 3, 1957, a man at a store called Kresge said he was certain he had seen the sisters. He claimed that they had come into his store and then spent quite a bit of time listening to Elvis Presley records.

One of the strangest and most eerie incidents happened late at night on January 14, 1957. At the home of Sandra Tollstan, a school friend of Patricia's, the phone range at midnight. The phone startled the parents of Sandra out of their sleep and they staggered to answer it. They picked up the phone and heard nothing but silence on the other end. Then the phone went dead. Suddenly, minutes later, the phone rang again. This time when Sandra's mother picked up the phone she heard a young girl on the other end whisper, "Is that you, Sandra? Is Sandra there?" She would say that the girl on the other end sounded frightened and desperate and they ran to wake their daughter. By the time Sandra got to the phone, however, the caller was gone. Ann Tollstan, Sandra's mother, told authorities that she was absolutely certain that the voice on the other end of the phone belonged to that of Patricia Grimes.

The city was in a panic. Parents were refusing to let their children wander out at night. If two girls could not even head out to an evening at the movies and return home safely, then the world had officially gone crazy. The search intensified. The public, press, and parents still held out hope that the two girls would be found alive and well. For about a month this went on. Then, all hopes were dashed on January 22, 1957.

A construction worker named Leonard Prescott had pulled over to the side of the road because he had caught a glimpse of something that seemed strange. At first, he thought it might have been a couple of mannequins that, for some reason, had been tossed beside the road. He was in a suburb of Chicago known as Willow Springs, on the relatively desolate stretch of road known as German Church Road. He parked his truck and got out, walking slowly towards the pale white forms lying in a ditch, like discarded trash, beside the road. As he got close, the horror dawned on him. Those were not store dummies. They were the nude bodies of two human girls.

Horrified, Prescott got to a phone and called the police. Soon the entire area was swarming with onlookers and police detectives. It was the bodies of Barbara and Patricia. They were nude, covered with a layer of ice and snow, and both were dead. The coroner was called and the bodies were taken away — not before dozens and dozens of detectives, reporters, and gawkers tramped and stomped all over the scene. Control over the crime scene rapidly vanished. What evidence might have been stepped on or walked away can never be known.

There seemed, at first, to be no concrete reason as to why the girls were dead. It was hoped that an autopsy would reveal what had happened. Instead, the findings only added to the controversy.

The medical examiners said that it was likely the girls had died on December 28, the very day that they vanished. This would mean that all of the sightings and the phone call that had come after that were not viable or to be believed. The medical examiner concluded that the girls had died from a combination of shock and exposure to the elements. The conclusion was that the girls had been tossed beside the road naked and died from the cold. The controversy was that the examiner seemed to come to this conclusion by eliminating all other possibilities.

This theory proved to be controversial even among those investigating the crime. One of the lead investigators, Harry Glos, felt that this conclusion was wrong. He believed that the girls had been alive when they were tossed onto the side of German Church Road and died of something else besides exposure. Furthermore, he felt that the thin layer of ice on their bodies indicated that their bodies were still warm when they were tossed beside the road. He also felt that they could not have been covered with the layer of snow that they found on the bodies until after January 7, 1957. Therefore, he felt it was not possible for the girls to have been killed and discarded before that date.

There were other mysteries that were not addressed by the autopsy. For example, there were a number of bruises on both of their bodies that were not explained. Also, both of the sisters had several puncture wounds, some of them very deep, and potentially done by a sharp object like an ice pick. These seemed to have been dismissed as not relevant, but to some investigators these were key elements to the crime that had not been explained.

Despite this, the investigators had no choice but to go with it. Glos may have disagreed, but the official story was that the girls had been dumped on the side of the road the same night that they vanished and died due to shock and exposure. Also, the medical examiner stated that neither girl was molested or sexually assaulted. Glos, however, said he felt that this was not true, and that Barbara, in particular, had been molested.

Investigators now had a murder on their hands. While the girl's parents grieved publicly and the city mourned with them, investigators began finding people who might know something about what happened to the girls. The funeral of the Grimes sisters was covered by the local press and the city came to a stand-still as they were laid to rest.

The first person who the police investigated was the man who reportedly was seen with the girls at a restaurant with a supposedly drunk Patricia. That man was Edward L. "Benny" Bedwell. He had reportedly been a dishwasher at the D&L Restaurant and was said to be with the two girls on the morning of December 30. He was brought in by the sheriff's men and questioned, and, at first, confessed to the crime. Then, however, he recanted, saying that he had been coerced by the sheriff's deputies, which was not out of the question, given the time that his arrest occurred. Back then, there were few rights for suspects brought in for questioning and tactics that would be considered abusive in this day and age were often employed by investigators. He was eventually cleared of the charges and released, although Glos would maintain that he felt Bedwell had something to do with this disappearance, if not their actual murder.

Another suspect was 17-year-old Max Fleig. He was brought in for questioning and then underwent a polygraph test. According to investigators, he failed that polygraph miserably. However, despite the general lack of laws governing the rights of suspects and those being questioned, it was illegal to perform a polygraph on someone underage. Thus, the authorities had nothing that they could use against him — this, despite the fact that he allegedly confessed to actually kidnapping the two girls. Since his confession was obtained illegally, it was "poisoned fruit" and could not be used to charge him. The police had no actual physical evidence that Fleig had kidnapped the girls or had any actual contact with them. They had to let him go, but he has remained a favorite suspect by the many hundreds of people who have gone back and reviewed the Grimes case over the years. Just a few years later, he ended up going to prison anyway when he was convicted of murdering another young girl in a completely unrelated case.

Another suspect was a 52-year-old man who worked as a pipe-fitter. What brought him to the attention of authorities was that he called them directly and said that he had had a dream that the girls' bodies would be found at 81st and Wolf. That turned out to be very near where the bodies were ultimately found on German Church Road. He was taken into custody and questioned extensively, but ultimately the investigators thought that he had nothing to do with the case and let him go.

Those were the three best suspects that the police had and, in each case, they did not have enough evidence to arrest and charge anyone. There have been many, many theories as to what might have happened to those girls and who they might have been mixed up with. One theory is that they ended up involved with men who wanted them to get into prostitution and that one of the girls balked at the idea and both were killed because they knew too much.

The case remains open to this very day. At the turn of the century, another murder that happened at almost the exact same time and involving the brutal rape and murder of three young boys was solved. The criminal who had committed that shocking crime was brought to justice. As such, it is still hoped that some clue or piece of evidence about the Grimes sisters will come to light and provide answers all of these years later. To date, however, that has not happened and the case remains one of the most frustrating of open cases still on the books.

Over the years, other legends have popped up. Some say that the section of German Church Road where the bodies were found is haunted. Houses that were in the area are now mostly abandoned, the residents having moved away years ago. Some claim to see ghostly girls standing beside the road, but other supposed sightings are even stranger. For example, many say they either see an old 1950s car traveling down the road, or hear the sound of a car come to a halt near the place where the bodies were found, a door open and close, and then the sound of a car peeling off into the night. Could it be the killer's car? It is just another of many mysteries surrounding the case of the Grimes sisters.

Chapter Ten
The Murder
of Valerie Percy

Charles H. Percy was a popular businessman in the Chicago area during the late '50s and early-to-mid-'60s. He had been working at the company Bell & Howell for years, slowly working his way up until he became their President. He was the epitome of the American dream for many. He had moved to the Chicago area from Florida as an infant and had been raised as a Chicagoan for most of his life. He was a part of the Chicago community and when he turned to politics in the mid-'60s, he seemed a shoo-in for whatever office he chose. Perhaps he could start out as a senator and work his way up from there, like he had at Bell & Howell, and eventually find his way into the White House.

He decided to run as a Republican candidate for Senator. This was in 1966, and he had the backing of none other than former President Dwight D. Eisenhower. He had previously attempted to run for Governor of the state of Illinois, but had narrowly lost to incumbent Otto Kerner.

Percy had a gorgeous family that photographed well and should have appealed to those looking for strong family values. One of the highlights of his life was his 21-year-old daughter, Valerie. She was pretty and blond and just the kind of person to also appeal to voters. However, in the midst of his run for senator, on the night of September 18, 1966, Charles Percy's life changed forever, and one of the most frustrating and baffling — and brutal — crimes in Chicago history occurred in Percy's own home.

The crime happened early in the morning on that fateful day. The sun was still below the horizon. The Percy family lived in a mansion that ran up against the vast blue expanse of Lake Michigan. It was hushed that morning, peaceful and calm. The hectic schedule of the campaign weighed heavily on Charles Percy and the rest of his family. But that morning, someone decided to break into their mansion. What happened next would shock even some of the most hardened criminal investigators.

The crime would not be discovered until later that morning. The killer was not only brutal, but efficient and silent. When Valerie's body was discovered it was covered in blood, brutalized to such an extent that she was barely recognizable. The police and paramedics were called, and when a doctor showed up to see if he could help, he would later tell the press that he had never seen a body so horribly attacked.

Valerie had been stabbed, multiple times; most of the stab wounds alone would have been fatal. The doctor then turned to the wounds around Valerie's head. In addition to the stab wounds, she had been bludgeoned around her head and shoulders. The left side of her face had multiple lacerations, indicating a frenzy on behalf of her killer. Her left eye was swollen shut, but her right eye was partially open. The doctor found a large clot of blood located on the back right side of her neck. Valerie had no pulse and she was not breathing. She was in bed as if she had been sleeping peacefully when the attack occurred.

At first, given the fact that it was a mansion that had been broken into, it was thought that a cat burglar was the culprit—except that Valerie's dresser, which contained jewelry and other valuables, had not been disturbed. Nothing was found missing in and around the home, either. No one else in the house had seen or heard anything and it seemed as if the killer had known exactly how to get to Valerie's room, as if he intended her to be the victim all along. Her twin sister, Sharon, was not disturbed. Did Valerie know who her killer was?

The Percys lived in what was considered one of the safest suburbs in and around Chicago. The area was known as Kenilworth. They lived on a large 3,000-acre estate. Valerie and Sharon were both 21, and there was a son named Roger, who was 19, another daughter named Gail, aged 13, and a son, Mark, aged 11. None of them had been robbed, saw anything, heard anything, or had been attacked that fateful morning.

For the local cops, this was a case well out of their league. The Kenilworth police were used to dealing with a few rowdy teenagers, the occasional burglary, but nothing like this brutal homicide. Since the town had been founded, seventy-five years before, not a single murder had been investigated by authorities there.

It was obvious from the start that this was not going to be a typical murder investigation. When Valerie's funeral was held, President Richard Nixon attended and J. Edgar Hoover, the head of the FBI, stepped in to offer help in tracking down Valerie's killer. It seemed that with that kind of spotlight in the case and that kind of investigative firepower focused on it, a killer would be found quickly and the case would be wrapped up. Sadly, that did not happen.

There were thousands of people investigated. Investigators looked at other break-ins that had happened in the area, pouring over details and looking for similarities. Charles Percy's political contacts, including his rivals, were also questioned and examined. Family friends and relatives were questioned. Police interrogated local mobsters, many of whom had elaborate mansions and homes on that side of town, and rounded up known burglary rings to question. They followed up hundreds, and then thousands, of tips that poured in from all over the city from concerned citizens who were sure that they knew something about the crime and who had committed it. All of it led nowhere.

There was nothing in Valerie Percy's life that indicated such a horrific and tragic ending was in store. Valerie and her twin, Sharon, had both attended school together, and were close and identical in most ways in their very early years. However, while still in grade school, they both decided that they did not want to be carbon copies of each other and would find their own identities. They no longer wore the same clothes and they moved into separate bedrooms.

The girls graduated from grade school in 1958. Both then attending the elite New Trier High School in north suburban Winnetka. They were close, but they had different friends and different interests. Sometimes, they came close to matching up, such as when both girls took advantage of New Trier's foreign exchange programs during their junior year. However, Sharon decided to go to Switzerland and Valerie elected to spend time in Paris. They both did very well in school and graduated in 1962.

Once again, they ended up deciding to go to different colleges. Sharon enrolled in Stamford, which took her all the way to the West Coast. Valerie decided to head to the opposite side of the country and attended Cornell, which is in New York state. Once again, both girls did very well at the universities and were very active with school activities and, by all accounts, were popular among their friends. They both graduated from their respective universities in 1966.

It was then that Valerie decided she was interested in politics, particularly her father's political run for senate. She returned home to work with his campaign. Her sister, Sharon, decided that she wanted to head out into the world and help others. She went to the Central African Republic to teach English courses. She did that for a while and then decided to return home to help out with the campaign by that Labor Day.

Sharon, meanwhile, had fallen in love with a man named Jay Rockefeller. He was the son of one of the most famous and wealthiest men in the country. It looked like Sharon and Jay were very much in love and talk of wedding bells was in the air that summer and fall, as the family helped with Charles' campaign. Valerie, at the time of her death, was not seeing anyone in particular, but had had several boyfriends and many young men had expressed their interest. Politics, meanwhile, had become her passion and she was wrapped up in helping with her father's campaign.

On the night before she was killed, Valerie spent a relatively quiet night at home. She had dinner with two friends and several members of her father's campaign. There was nothing strange about her behavior or anything else during that meal. She went to bed at 10 p.m.

83

Sharon, meanwhile, had a date with Jay that night. She had earlier borrowed one of Valerie's raincoats to use on her night out. Sharon came home at about 11:30 p.m. and went to her sister's room to say good-night and return the borrowed coat. She told authorities that Valerie was there, awake, and watching TV when she knocked on her door. They talked only briefly and then said good night. That was the last time anyone in Valerie's family saw her alive.

That morning, it was Valerie's step-mother who found her body. In fact, Loraine Percy was sleeping soundly in her bed that Sunday morning when a sound awoke her. It was the sound of breaking glass. It jolted her awake and she sat up in bed, listening. There were no another sounds, but something was worrying her. She got up and padded her way down the hall, her feet hushed on the thick carpeting. At first, she stopped at Sharon's door, listening. She heard nothing from behind the door, but then heard another sound from Valerie's room.

She hurried down the hall and opened Valerie's door. She was stunned to see a man hunched over Valerie's bed. The man held a flashlight, which shone its light over Valerie. In the brief seconds that Loraine Percy had a clear vision of what was in her step-daughter's bed, she saw that Valerie's body was covered in blood from the top of her head and most of the way down her torso. Her bed looked as if it had been painted in red. Later, after calming down and after the police arrived at their home to take statements, Loraine would say that she remembered that he was relatively short, about 5' 8" and maybe 160 pounds. She would also say that she remembered he had dark hair and was wearing a checked shirt. She would eventually remember enough to provide a police sketch artist with a description. The picture shows a man with a long narrow face and pointed chin, dark, close-cropped hair, and dark-rimmed glasses.

The intruder turned and looked at Loraine, shining his bright flashlight directly into her face and eyes. This made it nearly impossible for her to see him clearly. Loraine immediately turned and ran back to her room, pausing long enough to trigger a loud burglar alarm that pierced the night and sent the intruder out into the darkness. Apparently the intruder followed Loraine out of the room, through the house, down a spiral staircase, through the bottom floors, and out a set of French doors and into the night.

Loraine was screaming by this point, which woke Charles. Both Charles and Loraine ran back to Valerie's room. They felt for a pulse and found a faint one, but the sheer amount of blood made them panic.

One of the next door neighbors, awakened by the shrieking burglar alarm, went to their windows and out into their backyard. They would tell authorities that they saw no one running from he house, or anywhere near the Percy mansion. Just minutes later, their phone would ring. It was Charles Percy, asking if the husband, a doctor, could come over. Valerie was badly hurt. The husband put pants on and hustled over to the Percy house. He ran up the stairs and did what he could, but by that time, it was too late. He slowly made his way downstairs where the family in the house had gathered. He told them that Valerie was gone.

Police hoped that evidence gathered from around the property would lead them to a suspect. They also hoped that the autopsy and searching the body would reveal some sort of trace of the killer. They discovered that Valerie had been beaten at least four times with a small ball peen hammer, fireplace poker, or something with a conical head. She had also been stabbed in the head and neck fourteen times. They found bruises and stab wounds on her hands and arms, which indicated that she was not entirely asleep during the assault and had died fighting her attacker.

The police began an intensive search of the grounds. They discovered that the assailant had entered the home by cutting a screen. He had then used a glass cutter to cut out a section of glass on an interior window. The falling piece of glass, shattering on the floor, was what Loraine had heard and that had awakened her.

Once they had that figured out, the police began searching the vast property. They hoped to find more evidence that would lead to a suspect. They found a bunch of things on the lawn and across the grounds that they put into evidence, including a moccasin, a glove, a bayonet, a pocket watch, half of a pair of scissors blades, and a knife that had been rusted to the point of near uselessness. Any of them had the potential to be a lethal weapon. However, despite such an intense haul of evidence, none of it had anything that investigators could use and none of the sharp objects ended up being the ones that had been used on Valerie.

They found other evidence that they hoped would lead somewhere. Down on the beach, near the lapping blue waters of Lake Michigan, they found footprints, but they were nebulous and unclear. They also found a fingerprint that was clear on the piece of broken glass. They were able to find a palm print and more fingerprints on the door to Valerie's room and more evidence of prints on a railing on a stairway. Hair and fibers that were not from the house or Valerie's room were found scattered about her bedroom.

In a move that seemed designed to rub salt in the wounds, but in accordance with Illinois law, the crime warranted a coroner's inquest. That meant that the family had to march their way down to the coroner's office and tell their stories over again. What they ended up coming away with was that no one in Valerie's family had a motive for why anyone would so brutally murder their daughter. The inquest deliberated and analyzed what evidence they had and determined what seemed obvious: that it was a homicide and that there should be a full investigation.

The press was filled with images of the family. Charles Percy suspended his campaign for two weeks. Then he went back to work, campaigning hard for his senate seat. He ended up winning the election, surprising the incumbent Democrat, for the seat. He would serve for years faithfully as a senator.

Police began tracking down leads and tips. Hundreds of tips poured in from people who thought they knew something. Since the police had nothing else to go on, they were forced to track down each and every lead until exhausted, even if the lead seemed like it had come from a crank. Before long, despite such a promising beginning and despite being a case with such a high profile, the leads began to dry up. The police detectives were forced to move on to other cases. Over time, among the general public, the case vanished from sight and became forgotten as other more notorious and headline-grabbing murders and cases came up and caught the public's attention.

For some investigators, however, the case was never forgotten. Even as the task force assigned with keeping the investigation dwindled to four men, some police detectives continued to comb through the evidence, hoping to find something that might have been missed. Charles Percy himself put up a $50,000 reward for information leading the culprit in the murder of his daughter. That reward has never been claimed.

Over the years, many suspects have come to light. Investigators have tracked down those leads, but come up empty. It seems to be the case that comes back to haunt investigators and pops up in the press on the anniversary of the crime.

As for Charles Percy, he eventually retired. Years later, he was diagnosed with Alzheimer's. He eventually died, almost to the date of Valerie's murder, in his '90s. He died never knowing what happened to Valerie.

The case remains open to this day. The mystery endures.

Chapter Eleven
Al Capone and the
St. Valentine's Day Massacre

The St. Valentine's Day Massacre is one of the most famous incidents in the history of the mafia and within the history of Chicago's crime-ridden past. It has become synonymous with the 1920s, bootlegger/gangster era that, to this very day, often defines Chicago for most people. It is also synonymous with notorious gangland leader Al "Scarface" Capone. Most people probably think that this is a crime that was solved long ago, with the perpetrators sent off to prison. Heck, even Al Capone ended up in prison almost to the day he died, so he must have gone because of information that connected him to this brutal and infamous crime. If that's something you believe, however, you would be very wrong. Although many people take for granted that Capone masterminded the massacre, the fact remains that not a single gunman or gangster was ever arrested, prosecuted, or convicted for this notorious crime.

February of 1929 was a dangerous time in Chicago and a very dangerous time to be a gangster. The city was divided in two. On the north side of town, a man named George Clarence "Bugs" Moran controlled things. It was the time of Prohibition and the gangs in Chicago made their money by funneling illegal booze into the city and, from there, the rest of the country. It may have been illegal to own or drink alcohol, but the American appetite for booze seemed insatiable and that was never more evident than on the streets of Chicago. On the south side of the city, Alphonse "Al" "Scarface" Capone ran things with an iron fist. Even among the brutal gangsters who ran things out east, Al Capone was feared.

In between these two titans of crime, the soul of the city and the everyday lives of men and women of all ages hung in the balance. For years, throughout much of the '20s, the two gangs had been battling it out like armies in a war, trying to gain territory and, ultimately, gain control of all of the illegal booze rackets throughout the city of Chicago. There had been brutal shootings, stabbings, stranglings, murders, bombings, and other death and destruction on both sides. At times, innocents had been caught in the crossfire, but such were things in Chicago during the '20s. If you wanted to drink, you had to do so illegally and that meant dealing with the lowest of the low, like Capone and Moran.

Over the course of the years, Al Capone had been gaining and consolidating power. He was Italian, while Moran was Irish. That meant that the more powerful Italian mafia, based out east, had a horse in this race to gain power, as well. Throughout the years, Capone's methods had grown more brutal and more intense. He seemed invincible, not only having much of the money that went through the city at his fingertips, but being able to use his power and influence to buy politicians, judges, and more. There was actually a time when it was thought that if Al Capone had run for mayor of Chicago, he would have won. He was affable and appeared to be a regular working stiff to many. For a time, he was considered more of a lovable rogue by the general populace, rather than the brutal, murdering criminal he really was. He was thought to bring a needed service to the general hard-working people of Chicago, who just wanted to be able to work hard, earn a good wage, and have a drink when the work day was over.

Capone had been growing his territory. He wanted all of Chicago. Moran, however, had refused to back down or to join up with Capone and had declined to leave town. So, for months, a plan took shape that would, once and for all, eliminate Moran, his gang, and the north side Irish mob. With them gone, the city would, in truth, belong to one man, Alphonse Capone. It was decided that the event would happen during the heart of another brutally cold and snowy Chicago winter. In fact, St. Valentine's Day would be the day.

As for Capone, how much involvement he had in planning the events that occurred that day is still unknown. However, it was well known among gangsters that Capone took a very serious hand in controlling his city. He may have offered as much help as was needed, including helping to find the alleged gunmen who would commit his definitive act. Capone himself, meanwhile, would have the ultimate alibi. He would be thousands of miles away, lounging by his pool at his large estate in Florida. For many, though, Capone's shadow stretched all the way from the peninsula of Florida to the snowy streets of Chicago that day.

That morning, a group of gangsters, all of them members of Moran's gang, got together for another day of committing crimes and planning murders at 2122 North Clark Street on the north side of town. Their meeting place was a garage located there. Inside was a mechanic with his dog; he was working on cars and doing his job. The gangsters, meanwhile, met in the empty space, waiting for Moran himself to show up. He was supposed to be at this meeting, but was running late.

Meeting that morning were:

- Peter and Frank Gusenberg, both soldiers in Moran's army and known to be enforcers;
- Albert Kachellek, who was so high in the rankings of the Moran gang that he was considered his second-in-command — technically, he had retired from his life of crime, but was there to visit with Moran and the others that morning;
- Adam Heyer, a bookkeeper for the Moran gang;
- Reinhart Schwimmer, a gambling man, who liked to bet on horses and had once been optician who had become friends with Moran and members of his gang, but was not officially part of the gang; and
- Albert Weinshank, who ran a cleaning and dyeing operation that provided a front for Moran's "legal" business endeavors and who bore a very striking resemblance to Moran himself.
- Finally, as mentioned, there was the mechanic John May and his German shepherd Highball, who was tied to the bumper of one of the cars.

Things between the two gangs had been boiling for some time. Capone and his men had rubbed out the original leader of the North Side Gang, Dion O'Banion, by having gunmen shoot him down in his own flower shop. From that point forward, and over the course of a few years, everyone who took control of the gang found that his lifespan was very short. So far, Bugs Moran had managed to elude the bullet. However, Frank Gusenberg and his brother, Peter, had just the year before tried to gun down a prominent figure in Capone's gang, Jack McGurn. Thugs close to Moran had also been known to hijack trucks carrying illegal booze out of Detroit and meant for Capone's speakeasies on the south side.

Across the street several men looked out from windows and watched the garage. The plan was to get word to Moran that a shipment of whiskey was about to come in. They hoped to lure Moran to the garage, along with a few of his top lieutenants. It was hoped that by doing this, they would finally be able to cut off the head of the North Side Gang.

As the eyes watched, gunmen waited nearby for a signal. It is believed that a few of the gunmen, perhaps two, were dressed in policeman uniforms. Once they were sure that Moran was inside the building, the signal was to be given and they were to enter. They were to make it look like another police raid, and then open fire.

As it turns out, it was Weinshank who may have set everything in motion that morning. With his coat and hat on, turned up against the bitter Chicago winter, he looked almost exactly like Bugs Moran. In fact, Moran was running late that morning and would not arrive until events had transpired. However, to the eyes watching the garage, it looked like Moran had arrived, and the signal was given. The gunmen moved in.

They burst into the garage, shouting like cops. The North Side Gang held up their hands, shrugging their shoulders and wondering if they were going to be spending the day in jail until their releases could be secured. With Highball, the dog, barking away, the supposed cops lined the men up against the wall, their hands on the wall, and their backs facing the cops. It was then that the gunmen emerged; with Tommy Guns and at least one shotgun, they opened fire on the men who had their backs to them. In seconds, hundreds of rounds had been fired, riddling the wall with bullet holes and splattering the floor and walls with blood. The seven men collapsed to the floor in spreading pools of blood, a few of them dead already, but at least one still alive. The gunmen walked out, the two dressed like cops leading them with their hands up to make it look like they were being arrested in a raid. They got into cars and sped off.

For the residents of that neighborhood, an eerie silence fell over the garage. Several neighbors poked their heads out. Had they just heard gunfire? It was a garage, after all, and it could have been the backfire of a car. Several residents emerged from their homes, edging closer to the door, while inside Highball went on a barking and howling frenzy. It did not sound like everything was fine inside. Someone poked their head in and saw the bloody mess that was there.

Police arrived and found that most of the gangsters were dead. Not long after the police arrived, so did Moran. When he was told what happened, he fled the scene and hid out. By all accounts, he was never the same after that. In the end, the goal of the massacre had been achieved. For all intents and purposes, the North Side Gang never again posed much of a threat to Capone.

Tough guy Frank Gusenberg was still alive. The police made sure he was rushed to the hospital where doctors frantically tried to save his life. They did manage to stabilize him long enough for police to enter his room and try to question him. However, in true gangster tradition, Gusenberg held strong until the end. He told police, "Nobody shot me." He had twenty-two wounds caused by fourteen bullets that had entered his body. He succumbed to his wounds later that day, having never given up a single name of who had shot him or what had happened that morning.

Given the fact that the police knew that Moran's men had been hijacking the liquor shipments from Detroit, their initial focus was on a group called The Purple Gang. They were a group of Jewish hijackers, bootleggers, and gangsters who worked out of the Detroit area. They were also known for their brutality in keeping their territory. Police began circulating photographs of known members of the Purple Gang and began asking questions.

The city was shocked by what happened. At least one of the victims, the optician, was not even a gangster, just a man who happened to be friends with a few of Moran's gang. Those who had actually been sympathetic to the gangsters, determining that they were just providing a service that was needed and wanted by most average citizens, they felt that lining up seven of them against a wall and shooting them in the back was a bit much.

At first, the police thought they had some identification on the gunmen. Two landladies, Ms. Doody and Ms. Orvidson, who ran a boarding house just across the street from the garage, said that members of the Purple Gang had rented rooms from them just prior to the shooting. They picked out George Lewis, Eddie Fletcher, Philip Keywell, and his younger brother, Harry. However, when the police brought those men in for questioning, the two women suddenly began to waver in their identification of them. Police questioned the men, but they had no evidence and there was no proof to hold them and they were released.

There were many who fell for the ruse perpetrated by the killers. Many in the public thought that the police were responsible. Overall, however, it was believed that this was done by Capone's mob at the behest of Capone himself. The public backlash was sudden and probably surprising for Capone. People decided that they had had enough of the murders and that this one was particularly vicious. It also was very public, making headlines across the country and around the world. Since the gangsters relied on quiet to keep their businesses going, it was the kind of heat and attention that was not well appreciated among the criminal element.

Near the end of February, the police were summoned to the scene of a fire. Once they arrived, they found that a 1927 Cadillac Sedan had been taken apart and large portions were set on fire. They soon determined that the car had been used by the killers at the garage across town. The number on the engine block was traced to a car dealer on Michigan Avenue near downtown Chicago. The owner of the dealership told police that he sold the car to a man named James Morton who was from Los Angeles. The garage that was burning when the police arrived was rented to a man who gave the name Frank Rogers and his address as 1859 W. North Avenue, which was the location of the Circus Café. That café, in turn, was owned by a man named Claude Maddox, a former St. Louis gangster with ties to both Capone and the Purple Gang. That was as far as the police were able to connect the car and the fire to the murders.

Meanwhile, police thought that they had a good lead on one of the possible killers. A man who was driving a truck on that morning sideswiped what he thought, initially, was a police car. However, when he stopped and tried to see if anyone inside the car was hurt, a man wearing a police uniform waved him away. When he saw the mouth of the man wearing the police uniform, he noticed that the man was missing a front tooth. The same description of one of the men came from another source, a man who was the president of the Board of Education. There was only one man that police knew used a police uniform when committing his crimes and that was Fred "Killer" Burke.

Burke was a known criminal and robber. He and his partner, James Ray, were both known to don police uniforms when they committed their crimes. Burke was also wanted, and on the run, from a warrant for robbery and murder in Ohio. Police immediately began to search for both Burke and Ray as possible suspects in the massacre.

The Chicago police then began naming others who they thought might have been involved. John Scalise, Alberr Anselmi, Jack McGurn, and Frank Rio were all named as possible suspects. Scalise and Anselmi were known to be gunmen in the employ of Capone. Frank Rio was one of Capone's bodyguards. Police eventually leveled charges of murder against Scalise and McGurn for the massacre, but they never got to trial. In 1929, Scalise and Anselmi were murdered, reportedly by Capone, when Capone learned that the two were planning to have him killed to take over the South Side Gang. The police ended up having to drop charges against McGurn simply because they did not have enough evidence against him. McGurn, when he was released, took his girlfriend, the chief witness for the police, across state lines to marry her. Thus, she was now no longer required to testify against her spouse in accordance with the law.

As for Burke, the police finally were able to track him down. Police in Michigan raided a house owned by a man calling himself Frederick Dane. They did that because Dane had been in an accident where he rear-ended another vehicle. When Dane tried to get away, a patrolman jumped onto the running board of the car to get him to stop and he was shot three times. The patrolman later died and the driver of the car was driven off the road by police. It was later discovered that Dane was, in fact, Burke.

Back at Burke's house, they found a huge stash of money and a bulletproof vest. They also found two Thompson machine guns and a stash of pistols, shotguns, and other weapons. Michigan police notified the Chicago police of what they had found. Forensic tests proved that the two machine guns had been used in the massacre and that one of the guns had also be used in a murder in New York the year before.

However, when the prosecutors sat down and looked at the evidence, they didn't have much to obtain a conviction against Burke for the St. Valentine's Day Massacre. They had the best chance of nailing him for the murder of the patrolman. Burke ended up sentenced to life in prison for that murder and he died behind bars in 1940.

As for the case of the massacre, the leads grew cold. Public acceptance of Capone and his activities dwindled. His influence in Chicago began to erode. Eventually, the government would nail Capone for income tax evasion. He would end up in Alcatraz, one of the most notorious prisons in the country, until he started to behave strangely. He became disoriented and it was soon found he suffered from syphilis. Capone was eventually released and he retired to his Florida home, barely a shell of the man he had once been at the height of his powers, and he died quietly of a venereal disease.

As for the St. Valentine's Day Massacre, there have been dozens and dozens of theories about who did the killing and why. In the 1930s, a man arrested by the FBI for being part of the Barker Gang began confessing to crimes, including his participation in the massacre. Despite this, nothing was done by the FBI since, by then, most of the others he named as being part of the crime were long dead.

To this day, no one has ever been formally convicted of the crime. Even Capone, technically, was never charged, given the fact he was out of town and no one could ever prove he gave the go-ahead for the crime. It remains one of the most famous crimes in the history of Chicago, and arguably the most famous in the history of the Chicago Outfit, but it has never been officially solved. It remains an enduring mystery.

Chapter Twelve
The Smiley Face Killers

Hundreds of young men and women, all in their early 20s, die every year. Many of them die because of accidents and murders, some of them die from diseases, some just disappear or die due to mysterious causes that are never explained. However, there are at least two police detectives from the New York area who run under the theory that there is a gang of serial killers on the loose, looking for college-aged men to murder. Their method of murder is to drown them in local creeks, rivers, or streams. To make matters even stranger, they leave a chilling calling card behind. Near the crime scenes where these bodies are found is a spray-painted or hand-drawn image of a smiley-face with horns atop its head.

According to former New York City police detectives Kevin Gannon and Anthony Duarte, these killers have been some of the most prolific in American history. According to them, reports of young college-aged men wandering away from parties and bars into the wintry nights and then ending up drowned stretch from Minnesota, down through Wisconsin, across Illinois, and then spread out from nearly one corner of the country to the next. Could there really be roving gangs of killers out there, perhaps in vans or other large vehicles, operating primarily during the winter months, tracking and looking for drunken college students to then murder? Gannon and Duarte say *yes* and have been collecting data on these killings for years, but law enforcement from the Wisconsin and Minnesota police to the FBI say that there is no validity to the theory.

For residents in Chicago, the theory came home when a young man named Brian Welzien disappeared on New Years Eve, 1999. The young man had been seen partying and welcoming in the new millennium and century in downtown Chicago at the Ambassador Hotel. Late in the night, however, he had wandered away from his other friends, all of them around his age of 21, and staggered out into the cold Chicago night. Not long after that, and well into the next day as his friends recovered from their hangovers and the partying from the night before, his friends and family reported him as missing.

Welzien's disappearance prompted a huge search. The local Chicago media ran news stories that featured photos of his face. The newspapers put his face on the front page. Security cameras from inside the hotel showed him as he walked down hallways and out into the night. He appeared to be drunk, but there was no one seen with him in the videos. Where he might have gone, no one could say. He was from Elgin, a city about forty or so miles northwest of Chicago. He attended nearby Northern Illinois University and was a good student, even ending up on the Dean's list. He was majoring in Finance. His family and friends could not imagine who would want to do anything to him or where he might have gone.

Welzien was reported missing on January 1, 2000. The agonizing search for him went on for months. Then, on Saturday, March 18, the worst fears of his family and friends were confirmed. His body was found washed up on a beach near Gary, Indiana. He was autopsied and it was clear that he had died due to asphyxiation from drowning. There seemed to be no other evidence that would indicate that this was anything more than an accident. Thus, it was ruled a tragic accident. Brian, apparently, had gotten drunk, walked away from the hotel, down near the Chicago River and, for whatever reason, fell or dove into the water. The cold water would have sapped his strength fast and he would have drowned, his body eventually washing up all the way down the shores of Lake Michigan onto a beach in Indiana.

That should have been the end of it, but it wasn't. An investigative journalist in the Chicago area connected with other journalists about the death. The theory about the gang of serial killers had first hit the airwaves on *Good Morning America* back in 2008 and was presented by Kristi Piehl. She had done a story about the strange rash of drownings among young college-aged men across the Midwest and interviewed Gannon and Duarte. Had this death in Chicago been connected to that?

According to Gannon and Duarte, maybe as many as forty young men had been killed by this gang of serial killers. As of 2008, they were reportedly looking through more records of supposed accidental drownings and said that they had noticed deaths that fit the pattern in as many as eleven states. In each case, a seemingly fit, popular, smart student was at a party or bar. At some point, late at night, and usually in the winter months, they wandered away from the bar or party. At that point, they would not be seen again. Days later, their bodies would be found in some body of water, drowned. Gannon and Duarte said that they had evidence, in each case, that a wall, fence post, or some other landmark would be marked with a horned smiley-face image. For example, a horned smiley face was photographed, painted in red, in Aimes, Iowa in 1997. Beneath the smiling face were the words "Evil Happy Smiley Face Man" with many letters written backwards. To some, this was reminiscent of the Zodiac Killer who had terrorized the San Francisco area in the '60s and had taunted local police and media with handwritten messages that contained backwards letters.

Gannon and Duarte insist that there is a pattern and that their years of police experience have given them the training to spot it. It sounds terrifying, but is it true? According to Gannon and Duarte, they believe that there is more than one killer on the loose here. In fact, they believe it is an entire gang and that this gang may have inspired or spun off into smaller gangs that have perpetuated the crimes, spreading them out further than they were originally. Again, it sounds terrifying, but could it be true? The FBI says that this is wild fantasy and that there is not a bit of truth to the entire theory.

Even now, entire websites are dedicated to finding this supposed gang of serial killers who target college-age young men and drown them. The sites continue to look for patterns in the killings. Some have even suggested that certain killings in certain areas of the country, when plotted out on a map and then linked together with lines, form smiley-faces. Others insist that other patterns and clues have been formed.

As for law enforcement, however, the incidents, including the one in Chicago, are all just tragic accidents. In each case, they repeatedly say that a young man simply went out on a cold winter's night, having had too much to drink. When he wandered away from the party and got near water, he drunkenly fell in. The fact he was drunk combined with the ice cold water simply made it impossible for the victim to swim or struggle against the tide, and they died.

There have even been accusations thrown against the two detectives who brought the theory into the public eye. Some say that they have pestered and disturbed family members to champion their cause, when their cause is some kind of monetary gain or a modicum of fame. Others have stated that families who once believed that their sons were involved with this gang of serial killers have now changed their minds. At the same time, people say that the two detectives continue to prey on these families even when the evidence mounts that their sons died because of an accident, in order to keep the story going and the theory alive.

Most importantly, law enforcement, including the FBI, have stated that some of the so-called evidence is spurious at best. For example, some say that the supposed smiley-face graffiti pointed to by those who espouse the theory are not really close in proximity to where the supposed crime took place and nowhere near where the bodies have been found.

So, on that New Year's Eve did a young man in Chicago meet a gang of serial killers? Did they target him because of his apparent age and the fact he was drunk? Did they drag him down to the Chicago River and then drown him? Or was it another tragic accident? Did the young man simply walk away from friends after having too much to drink, wander down by the river, and then stumble in? The Chicago River's current is known to be strong and, given the cold and a young man in an inebriated state, it would have been hard for him to get help or swim to shore.

The world may never know for sure. As of right now, no solid evidence proving the existence of the Smiley-Face Killers has ever been found. Some insist that the evidence is overwhelming. The FBI says that it's just wishful thinking and finding connections and links where there are none. Until a definitive piece of evidence is found, it's impossible to say for certain which is correct and which is a theory.

Chapter Thirteen
The Sad Tale of Elsie Paroubek

It was the spring of 1911 in the city of Chicago. The city, like so many large cities, had always been an amalgamation of a variety of nationalities that survived between borders drawn by politicians. The various immigrant populations tended to attract more of their countrymen and women and form tight-knit neighborhoods and cliques that allowed them to keep their same cultural traditions and even speak the same language. Chicago has a Chinatown, Little Italy, Greek Town, Korea Town, Little India, and more. Chicago is also a city filled with eastern bloc country immigrants from Russia, Poland, and other territories that were, at one time, part of the Soviet Union.

Little Elsie Paroubek lived in such a neighborhood. Her parents were Czech. She was a bright-eyed little girl with a mop of light-colored hair and dazzling blue eyes that stood out as if she were surprised. On the morning of April 8, 1911, she was 10 years old. What she did not know, what no one in her family could have known, was that on this morning, she was about to cause a search that would encompass three states, from Illinois up to Minnesota.

The Paroubek family was not a wealthy one. Elsie's father, Frank, had been born in the area of the Czech Republic known as Bohemia in 1867. Her mother had also been born in Bohemia, in 1869. Frank had moved to the U.S. when he was 15, but returned to Bohemia between the years of 1882 and 1892. He then married Karolina in 1892 in Bohemia. They both returned to the U.S. where Frank worked as a painter, while Karolina took care of the home and kids.

Elsie awoke that morning and told her mother that she was going to walk to a nearby neighborhood woman's home. This woman was a family friend known to Elsie as "Auntie," but her real name was Mrs. Frank Trampota. She only lived around the corner, and Elsie and her family knew her well. This was at a time when children routinely were allowed to wander all over their neighborhoods without their parents worrying too much. Nothing seemed strange about her request and her mother had no trepidation about allowing her to go.

Along the way, Elsie ran into her cousin, 9-year-old Josie Trampota. Josie and a bunch of other neighborhood children were gathered around a corner listening to an organ grinder. They stood there and watched for some time, and they even followed him when he moved to a different corner across the street, like a kind of pied piper. The organ grinder eventually moved on, with the children following him, including Josie, but Eslie stayed behind, apparently intending to continue with her original intent, which was to head to her aunt's home.

Later, Elsie's mother decided to head over to Auntie Trampota's home to see where her little girl was. She was not concerned and hoped to visit with Trampota, as well as pick up Elsie. When she got there, however, she was surprised to find out that Auntie Trampota had never seen Elsie. Elsie had never shown up.

Initially, it was thought that gypsies had taken Elsie. A wagon said to contain them, mostly likely Irish Travelers, was seen in the neighborhood before Elsie vanished. Also, one neighbor said that they saw a gypsy wagon traveling down the street, near where Elsie was last seen, and that two women on the wagon appeared to be holding a young girl. Elsie's father made an offer of his entire life's savings as a reward. That amounted to about $50, about $1,165 in today's economy.

The Irish Travelers had been in the neighborhood for some time prior to Elsie's vanishing. They had set up a camp nearby and one of the wagons at the camp had suddenly pulled up stakes and left the morning the little girl vanished. The story then gained credence because another young girl named Lillian Wulff, had vanished four years prior from her home. It was discovered that she had been kidnapped by gypsies. She was found after being missing for four years amidst a camp of gypsies. This gave hope to Elsie's family that maybe Elsie was still alive and Lillian Wulff began to advise police about how to approach the gypsies and how to possibly get Elsie back, if she were still alive.

A police inspector accompanied Frank to an area about forty-three miles south of Chicago, in an area known as Volo, Illinois. It was there that they believed they might find the gypsy wagons and, in particular, they hoped to find the wagon that had taken Elsie. Residents, upon hearing about the case of the missing child, had notified police that there was a camp near Volo that contained a number of gypsy wagons and that a young blond-haired girl was seen amidst them appearing stupefied. When Frank and the police inspector arrived, they tried to search the gypsy wagons, but as soon as they started entering the wagons the various gypsies pulled up stakes and left the area.

As for a motivation, there was not much to go on. The Irish Travelers, or gypsies, were feared in many communities. Prejudices abounded against these people because of their ways of living and moving from town to town, surviving by panhandling, pick-pocketing, and other methods were considered something to fear. The police inspector,

The Sad Tale of Elsie Paroubek

Stephen Healey, told the press that gypsies had a fondness for blond-haired girls with blue eyes and that Elsie was an irresistible choice for them.

The community that surrounded the Paroubek's came to their aid. The Czech community rallied around the family to offer them support. All Czech-speaking police officers in the city were ordered out of uniform and into undercover work in and around the neighborhood to look for clues and people who may have seen Elsie. Inspector Healey also ordered that several local waterways and canals be dredged in case the little girl in her red coat had wandered into the waters and drowned.

All across the city, the families in Chicago worried for their children and encouraged their kids to try and find Elsie. For example, one teacher at a local school, Ella Flagg Young, encouraged her children to form groups and try searching for Elsie while they were out on spring break. The search began to expand beyond the city of Chicago, encompassing the rest of the state of Illinois and then into Wisconsin.

Frank Paroubek, meanwhile, was desperate for information. He consulted a local psychic and asked for help. This psychic responded by saying that she had a powerful feeling that Elsie could be found in Argo, Wisconsin. At that point a Chicago politician, in a grand gesture, ordered a bunch of local Chicago officers to the location where the psychic indicated they could find Elsie, and they searched for her. But found nothing.

After that, the sightings of a little blond girl in a red outfit began to grow and increase. The police, frantically searching for leads and hoping to find the little girl still alive, had to follow up on each and every one of these reported sightings. Soon the entire investigation went from southern Illinois into northern Wisconsin, then into Minnesota, and back to Chicago. All of these investigations came to nothing.

To make matters worse, Frank Paroubek began receiving letters. They were insulting and cruel letters, claiming terrible things had been done to Elsie. Detectives tracked down these letters and came away with nothing, not even a suspect.

The reward for information leading to Elsie began to increase. In addition to the money from his savings, community leaders offered their monetary support. Soon the reward was up to $500, an astronomical sum in those days. Eventually, the city of Chicago offered to pass a resolution in the city council that would raise additional funds to create an even larger reward.

Investigators were completely swamped. Anyone within three states of Chicago who had seen a little girl with blond hair or a red coat, or anyone who had seen the Irish Travelers or gypsies was calling the police. They all thought that they had seen the little girl. With each phone call, police had to send detectives to investigate and each time the

little girls' parents had their hope renewed that something was going to happen that would bring their little girl home. Each time they were disappointed and crushed.

Then, the worst news imaginable came just two days after Elsie vanished. An electrical engineer named George Scully and several other employees at the Lockport, Illinois, power plant thought that they saw a body floating in the water of a drainage canal nearby. The water was deep enough that they had to use a boat to get to the small figure they could see beneath the murky water. They sent out a boat and recovered the body. The employees at the power plant had no idea about Elsie and they had no clue if it was her. They sent the body to an undertaker to do more research and the undertaker felt that the body before him matched the description of Elsie.

The undertaker contacted the Chicago police. The Chicago police detectives then had the sad task of notifying the parents of little Elsie. According to police, Elsie's mother, Karolina, cried out, "Me drahe ditte!" — which translates to "My dear child" — and collapsed into a fit of tears. She begged police to tell them that they were wrong and that her child was still alive. They were both brought to the undertaker and asked to view the body. Elsie's father said that he thought the body before him resembled Elsie, but in his shock, he felt that her mother would be able to identify her better. The hysterical Karolina was brought before the body and had to admit that the figure before her was her child.

Frank Paroubek angrily told the press that he still felt that it was the gypsies who had kidnapped his daughter. He also told them that he felt they had murdered her when the police began asking them questions, out of fear of being caught. At the same time, a report came out that the little girl had been suffocated, and that was soon reported as fact. It was theorized that someone had put their hand over the little girl's mouth and nose and suffocated her in that way.

As for the Paroubek family, they were in mourning. Karolina told a judge that she and her husband had spent all the money they had paying for the investigation. The judge wrote her a check for $25 and promised her more. Word spread that her parents did not have enough money to bury her and donations poured in from family and friends and concerned citizens.

On May 12, 1911, little Elsie Paroubek was laid to rest. Her funeral was held at her parent's home and a local church, as was often the custom at the time. Somewhere in the neighborhood of 2,000 to 3,000 people attended her funeral. Hours before the ceremony was to begin, the front and back yards of the Paroubek family were filled with mourners.

Chicago's police chief made a big public display about the case. He vowed to put every single police officer he had on the case to track down Elsie's killer. More government officials stepped forward, even petitioning the governor, to increase the reward offered for information leading to the killer or killers. The reward was now $500, a staggering amount.

One of the suspects in the case was a man known as Joseph Konesti. He was a hobo, hermit, and pan-handler. He had a hut set up near the drainage canal where Elsie's body was found and he had a reputation for, supposedly, enticing little girls down to his hut. When Konesti found out he was a suspect in the killing, he threw himself in front of a train, only to then have his name cleared a few days later.

On May 15, Frank Paroubek came forward and said that a man he did not know or recognize had approached him and said he had seen Elsie on Kedzie Avenue on April 8. This would have been days after the gypsies had supposedly taken her. Detectives were dispatched and asked to find this man. The last time it was known that Elsie was alive, she had been walking towards the canal in order to head toward her aunt's home. Now some detectives were thinking that maybe Elsie's death was not a murder. Some thought she might have just wandered down to the canal and fallen in, making this a tragic accident rather than something more notorious. Elsie's parents, however, remained convinced that someone had taken and murdered their daughter.

Frank and Karolina reported to police that they had once taken in a boarder. Police threw a dragnet around the southwest side of Chicago to try and find the man and question him. The man who reportedly talked to Frank on the street and the writer of the insulting notes that had been sent to his home were never tracked down and questioned.

Just two years later, near the anniversary of Elsie's disappearance, her father died. He was only forty-five years old and many said he was never the same after what happened to his daughter. Her mother, Karolina, lived until 1927. When Frank and Karolina died, they were buried in the same cemetery, on either side of little Elsie.

As for what really happened to Elsie Paroubek, no one knows for sure. The case faded into the past, despite the intense coverage it got at the time. Was she murdered by a band of gypsies who were out to kidnap blond-haired, blue-eyed little girls? Or had she simply wandered off her intended track to her aunt's home and fallen into the canal where she was later found? Either way, she was dead, and her parents wanted answers. Sadly, they never got those answers and the cause behind the death of Elsie Paroubek is still unsolved and unknown.

Chapter Fourteen
The Lane Bryant Murders

Tinley Park is a relatively quiet suburb on the south side of Chicago. Although the south side of Chicago has a notorious past, the suburbs that surround that area are just like suburbs you would find anywhere, in any city. Tinley Park is probably best known to most Chicagoans as the location of a popular outdoor music venue today known as the First Midwest Bank Amphitheatre. Beyond that, there is not much there that many would find different or spectacular. There are family homes and shopping malls, grocery stores and strip malls. In one of those strip malls is a store common among mall-goers; the store is called Lane Bryant.

The store is a relatively popular one across the country. It specializes in fashionable dresses and clothing for women who are more full-figured than your average magazine or catalog model. It is a clothing store just like any other clothing store and nothing that anyone, walking past the glass doors and windows, would bother to take a second glance at, were they to be walking past at that particular moment. It's the same kind of retail outlet that staffs a mix of young and old to work the floors and the cash register. There are young people who are trying to earn money for college or spending purposes. There are older people who have been in retail for years working there as managers and perhaps in a part-time capacity to earn extra money to make ends meet. It is a warm, friendly kind of place where no one thinks of anything bad happening. It's the kind of place where workers, therefore, might let their guard down.

What no one could possibly have known on the very cold day of February 2, 2008, was that the name of Lane Bryant and the name of Tinley Park was about to make national headlines. What no one could possibly imagine is how that quiet, unassuming store could become a house of horrors that would scar the community for years. What no one could ever imagine is that one of the worst cases of mass murder would occur behind its doors and remain, to this day, one of the worst unsolved murders in the country.

It was still relatively early in the shopping day and the crowd was fairly light, necessitating only a part-time employee and a store manager to handle the store. Inside were four customers, a part-time employee, and the store manager. Then, as the customers stood around making their final purchase decisions or paying for their clothes, a man walked in. It was, generally speaking, strange to see a single man walk into the clothing store that was, very obviously, meant to appeal to women. However, it was entirely possible that he knew someone at the store, or perhaps his wife or girlfriend worked there or was a shopper. Instead, this man pulled a gun and everything changed for the lives of those in the store and the lives of their families.

The six women were ushered into a room in the back of the store. The store itself was robbed and those in the store were robbed of money and other valuables. The victims probably hoped that this was all that was going to happen. Instead, the gunman/robber opened fire on the defenseless women. By the time the gunfire stopped, leaving only echoing sounds and the smell of burned gunpowder in the air, five of the six women were dead. The sixth, the part-time employee, was wounded, but alive.

Dead were Connie Woolfolk, 37, of Flossmoor, Susan Szafranski, 22, of Oak Forest, Carrie Hudek Chiuso, 33, of Frankfort, Jennifer Bishop, 34, of South Bend, Indiana, and the store manager Rhoda McFarland, 42 of Joliet, Illinois. The name of the surviving part-time employee has never been released to the media out of fear that the robber might try to track her down and finish the job he started that morning.

Police were called at 10:45 a.m. Arriving to find the grisly scene, they transported the survivor to the local hospital for treatment of her wounds. When she was conscious enough, she was able to provide them with a description of the gunman.

She said he was a black man with thick hair done up in corn rows. She also stated he had a receding hairline and one braid that lay along the right side of his face, dangling to about cheek-level. At the end of that braid there were four light-green beads attached for decoration.

Police shut down the store and the mall, since it was thought that the gunman might still be there. After a thorough search, however, it was determined that the gunman had left the premises. The mall was re-opened. The store itself, however, remained closed and was eventually closed permanently.

The story soon made national headlines. The Chicago area was still trying to heal the wounds of a seemingly similar incident that took place on the opposite side of town. In that case, in the northwestern suburb of Palatine, workers and customers in a Brown's Chicken fast-food restaurant were ushered into the walk-in fridge at that store and shot. It took years for that crime to be solved before the girlfriend of one of the gunmen finally came forward and turned in her boyfriend.

The national newspapers carried the story along with the police drawing of the alleged gunman. The national news organizations featured the story. Even the man who would become President of the United States, Barack Obama, came forward and made a statement about the tragedy in Tinley Park. It was hoped that someone would come forward with information immediately that would lead to a resolution in the case.

The parent company of Lane Bryant, Charming Shoppers, Inc., put up a $100,000 reward for information that would lead the capture of the man who had killed five people that morning. Then, on February 6, 2008, the same organization announced the creation of The Lane Bryant Tinley Park Memorial Fund dedicated in honor of the five women who had died in their store. The company also offered to pay for the funerals.

The survivor lived in fear. Her name was never released, but she did speak to the media on condition of anonymity. She told the press that she was afraid all the time. She felt that she was marked and that the man who had so coldly gunned down all of them was still out there, looking for her, and hoping he would get the chance to finish her off for good.

Although the police have said, many times, that they do not consider the case a cold case, the fact is that no new clues have come forward that the police have made public. There has been no arrest in the case. There has been no indictment. There has been no trial. Every year, on the anniversary of the crime, the media in Chicago mentions that the case is still open and provides the description of the alleged gunman and shows the police drawing. At this point, however, it seems that whoever walked into that store that bitterly cold February day got away with one of the most cold-blooded and vicious mass murders in the history of Chicago and, perhaps, the nation.

To this day, it remains one of the most notorious unsolved crimes in the nation, let alone the Chicago area. Residents of Tinley Park still live in fear and wonder if someone within their midst might have been the gunman who brutally shot down six people that day, killing five of them. The woman who survived, reportedly shot in the neck, still worries that she will be found, and police, still searching, are hoping for the tip or the clue that could bring the man to justice.

Chapter Fifteen
The Murder of Kevin Clewer

As has been mentioned elsewhere in this book, the city of Chicago, like so many large cities, is divided up into various sections. While there is no hard and fast rules that people of each persuasion and ethnicity live in just those sections, it seems as if like-minded people congregated to these areas of town. Thus, you have sections of the city that are dedicated to each ethnicity and country, and you have sections of town that bring people together because of their sexuality. One area of the north side of the city is rife with bars and clubs that cater to homosexual men and women. Sometimes this part of town is referred to as "Boys Town," although it has little to do with the more famous version of that title.

Kevin Clewer was a young handsome man of 31 in March of 2004. He lived on the north side of town, not exactly within the "Boys Town" area, but not far. He was a handsome gay man with dark hair, soft eyes, and an easy smile. And on March 24, 2004, he would become one of the Chicago gay community's most notorious unsolved crimes.

Of course, any crime involving a minority group can be charged with emotion. Are the police not investigating things with enough diligence because the person belongs to that certain minority group? Are prejudices that seem inherent within the Chicago Police Department keeping the investigation stagnant? Do the politicians and residents of certain areas of the city want the case to be forgotten?

The fact remains, however, that Kevin Clewer was alive and well on the morning of March 24, and brutally murdered before the day was over. He had a family. He had friends. He was well-liked by the many people who knew him. And whatever his sexual orientation, and no matter how people felt about that, he did not deserve what happened to him that horrible day.

It was Kevin's father who found his body that day. He came to Kevin's apartment, located at 3444 N. Elaine Place in Lakeview. Lakeview is a very bustling community with huge high-rise apartment and condo complexes that border Lake Shore Drive with a spectacular view of Lake Michigan. In between those apartments are large homes populated by families, many of them young, crowded against each other on narrow streets. It is true city living. But the residents are metropolitan in many ways. They walk or ride bikes to places, did away with their cars whenever possible, and carried their groceries home with them every day rather than stocking up for a week and transporting them by car.

The area is also dotted with numerous night clubs, bars, pool halls, and night spots. The young and gorgeous from all over the city often met up late at night in Lakeview and nearby Lincoln Park. This often meant that they then hopped from one bar to the next, getting more and more drunk, and more and more rowdy the later the night went on.

When Kevin's father knocked on his son's door that day, there was no answer. When he used his key and opened the door, he had no idea the horror that would be awaiting him when he went inside. His son had been stabbed to death. Blood spattered the walls, the ceiling, and coated the floor upon which he lay. The coppery smell of blood filled the air.

The police were called. In 2003, in Lincoln Park, another gay man, this man a theatre director, named Brad Winters, had been stabbed to death in his home. Police, and residents, when word got out about what had happened to Kevin, were worried that they might have a serial killer in their midst. Police did what they could to try and calm those fears, assuring everyone that they felt it was a separate case and that there was no evidence that a serial killer was the culprit, but it did little to assuage those fears of residents.

Police began to question Kevin's friends. They discovered that the night before his murder, he had been visiting the bars and clubs up and down Halsted Street, right in the middle of Boys Town. He had been seen, it was reported, with a man that night. Friends gave a description of this man to police and a sketch was widely circulated around the city — and, in particular, around Kevin's neighborhood. It was thought that this mysterious stranger's name was "Fernando."

He was described as being about 5'7" tall. He had dark hair, curly, and hanging down a bit over his face, just above his eyes. He had a slim, but athletic build with darker skin. He was reported to speak with a Spanish or some other European-Spanish accent.

And that was as far as police, and the investigation, ever got. Soon after, all of the leads dried up. The case grew cold, except for the family and friends of Kevin Clewer. His family still reunites when they can, trying to generate more press coverage and renew interest in the case. The police say that the case is still open, but they have no new leads and nothing else to go on. If "Fernando" does exist, he has never been found and no one has turned in information leading to his arrest.

As for the residents of Lakeview, they still wonder if a serial killer had been at work. In the prior murder, the man who was found stabbed to death in his home had also been in the bars on Halsted the night before he was killed. Some even said that they thought they had seen him in the company of a man that matched Fernando's description, but that could never be corroborated.

Some others looked at other unsolved murders and wondered if there were others that fit the pattern. For example, on June 29, 2004, a man who ran a Cubs souvenir store near Wrigley Field was found murdered in his home just blocks from where Clewer's apartment had been. Then, in October of that same year, the body of another man was found in his apartment in Edgewater. Friends said he frequented many of the bars that Clewer and Winters were seen in.

Police wondered if those two extra murders were connected as well. However, they were soon able to find culprits in each, and they were different culprits. They closed those two cases and determined that they were unrelated to each other, and not related to the deaths of Clewer or Winters.

The similarities of the two murders are striking. In both cases, neither home nor apartment showed signs of a force entry. Thus, the two men must have known their killers, and let them in willingly. Still, the question remains, who did it? Why?

Emotions still run strong in the gay community in Chicago about the case of Kevin Clewer. Many still feel that his killer is out there and perhaps even still in the Chicago area. They feel that the police need to be doing more to solve his case. They feel that Kevin Clewer could be forgotten unless they do what they can to keep his memory alive, and keep his case top-of-mind.

To this day, however, not a single suspect has been brought in or charged in the brutal murder of Kevin Clewer. His case remains unsolved and open within the files of the Chicago Police Department.

Chapter Sixteen
The Haymarket Square Riots

For some, it may come as a surprise to see this incident included in the list of unsolved mysteries. This is a famous incident that took place all the way back in 1886 in the history of Chicago. Eight people were arrested for the crime. Seven were sentenced to death and one to life in prison. Four men ultimately went to the gallows and another committed suicide by actually holding a dynamite cap in his mouth and lighting the fuse. Surely this means that this is a solved crime, correct? The fact is, the answer is *not quite*.

In 1886, things among average working men were quite different than things are today. Most workers worked all but one day a week. They also routinely worked long hours, with little time left for caring for their families—or anything else. Life was hard for the average working man. So much so that there were many who wanted that to change.

In May of 1886, one of the biggest workers' rights movements in the country was the fight for the eight-hour work day. Although that is common today, it was unheard of at the time. There were early forms of workers' unions and many a businessman considered them communistic and promoting anarchy. So many people were involved in the workers' rights movements that they adopted that name and called themselves anarchists. They wanted the average workers to be in control of their lives and their work, not the bosses and managers who ran the businesses. The managers at the top of those business food chains thought that the eight-hour work day would be the death of business in America. They said that the eight-hour work day would be impossible for businesses to maintain and remain competitive. As such, management in the largest companies in the country very actively did what they could to prevent unions and to prevent their workers from amassing or getting what they demanded.

Often times the methods used by the managers were harsh and cruel and violent. They frequently hired the Pinkerton Detective Agency to break up strikes. The Pinkertons were famous for their ability to track down criminals, but they were also an early version of a national police force. They protected key politicians, such as the President, and they could be hired out as bodyguards or guards to try to protect the businesses of some of the wealthiest people in the country. And they were not afraid to use truncheons and guns and other weapons to try and break up strikes and to strike fear into the workers.

Since the U.S. had ended the Civil War, the industrialization of the country had grown by leaps and bounds. As the country came back together, the country also began to expand its reach around the world. The U.S. was becoming a major industrial force for the rest of the world, and this not only attracted immigrants, it also increased the demand put on those workers by the management. The management at the top of these companies were making money that had never been seen before in the country, and they did not want troublemakers doing things to put that wealth in jeopardy.

The activists were very dynamic in and around Chicago. During that time, Chicago was a boom town. Industry was exploding all around the city. Large numbers of immigrants, many of them from Germany and Bohemia, were coming to Chicago. They were hoping to find and make better lives for themselves, but they found harsh working conditions and treatment from their bosses. They were expected to work all hours and for as many days of the week as their bosses required, receiving meager pay and little else. They were considered a means to an end, and that end was to get richer at the top of the corporate ladder. Most of the immigrants made about $1.50 a day for their efforts and their working conditions were deplorable and dangerous.

The problem was that the people who were championing changing the conditions for the workers were the anarchists. They were a revolutionary group and well known for having an armed military division of their group. They were also known to carry and store guns, to study explosives, and to specialize in making bombs. This meant that as soon as the anarchists came to town and started stirring up trouble, they were immediately considered a lethal threat and were often treated as such.

A group of workers' supporters met in early 1886. They were called the Federation of Organized Trades and Labor Unions. They began to champion the eight-hour work day and they decided that May 1, 1886 (May Day) would be the day when massive demonstrations would be held by workers across the country. Workers were encouraged to walk off their job and strike, and to meet in large numbers in the biggest cities around the country. This caused fear among the bosses, but the workers were eager to show how many they numbered and how powerful they could be.

When May 1 came, workers went on strike. The numbers in the various cities varied depending on who was reporting the story and whether or not they supported the workers' causes. In New York,

it was estimated that 10,000 workers struck; in Detroit, about 11,000 and in Milwaukee, about 10,000 workers showed up for a rally and demonstration demanding the eight-hour work day. In Chicago, it was estimated that at the center of the city's demonstration, anywhere from 30 to 40,000 people rallied and demonstrated. There were also numerous smaller demonstrations around the city, and it was felt a total of 80,000 workers went on strike in the Windy City, although not all at one time.

There was also a huge gathering and march that traveled right down Michigan Avenue in the heart of downtown Chicago. Leading that march was a well-known activist and anarchist named Albert Parsons. He was the leader of the International Working People's Association. He was at the head of the march, along with his wife and his children.

With the success of the marches in Chicago on May 1, it soon became the epicenter of the eight-hour day movement. On May 3, another series of rallies were held. This time a group of workers met right near the McCormick Harvesting Machine Company plant. Since February, unionized molders had been locked out of the plant. The molders and workers who were on strike had been demonstrating outside the plant, only to find themselves under attack by the Pinkertons. The strikers had remained solid, however, despite the attacks and stuck to their belief in an eight-hour day. This had made them well known and respected by other workers in the area.

The McCormick Company decided to bring in strikebreakers. These were people, often just as desperate for work as the striking workers themselves, trucked in to take over jobs held by the unionized striking workers. By the time the May Day rallies were held, the trucks bringing these workers into the plant were being guarded by over 400 guards, all of whom were armed. On May 1, about half of those strikebreakers actually defected and joined their unionized brothers on the picket lines. Despite this, the strikers continued to hurl things at the trucks, yell and scream and harass the strikebreakers as they were trucked in.

Appearing at the rally on May 3, another well-known anarchist appeared. His name was Albert Spies. He showed up and began encouraging workers to hold their ground. He encouraged them to fight back against the police who guarded the strikebreakers and the strikebreakers themselves. He also encouraged them to fight back against the Pinkertons. Tensions were high that day and when Spies and others showed up to encourage the strikers, tensions got even higher.

At the end of the work day, a bell sounded. Spies begged the strikers to stay where they were, but they surged forward toward the gates of the plant to confront the strikebreakers. It appeared as if violence was imminent. Police opened fire on the crowd. Two workers were killed in the subsequent gunfire and melee.

Workers were outraged, and the anarchists particularly so. Spies told the press that he felt that this was the next likely step on behalf of the management. They would vilify the workers in order to condone the violence against them. He argued that the managers would exploit the workers all the more and execute more of them. Fliers were printed and handed out, asking that the working men of the city grab their weapons and appear for a rally at an area known as Haymarket Square, which was a bustling commercial center located at Randolph and Des Plaines streets.

When Spies saw the first printing of the fliers, he was not happy. He did not want there to be violence. He said he would not speak unless any comment asking for the workers to show up armed be removed. The fliers were destroyed, with only a few hundred being distributed. Thousands more were printed asking the workers to show at Haymarket Square. The fliers were printed in English and German, the two predominant languages for the workers that the anarchists and workers' rights people were trying to reach.

It was May 4 and a cloudy sky opened up to let a light rain fall on the rally organizers and the striking workers who arrived at Haymarket Square that night. The evening started out with a festive feeling to it, almost like a block party. It started peacefully and a horse cart was brought to one end of the square. From here, the organizers planned to give speeches to rally the workers and proclaim that their cause was just, while the cause of management and the police was unjust. Nearby, at the outskirts of the square, a large number of police had gathered. Rumors had circulated that people were encouraged to bring guns and explosives to the meeting and a large number of police were dispatched by the Chicago city authorities to keep order. When the police saw who was speaking and the relatively calm atmosphere, they held back. At first, all seemed to be amused by the spectacle and no threat was detected.

Spies was well-known in the area and to workers. Charismatic and passionate, he was also the editor of the German-language newspaper *Arbeiter-Zeitung (Worker's Times)*. He was passionate about protecting the working man and he was known for his fiery and intense speeches. He was the first that night to mount the horse cart and walk to the edge to speak. Before him stood a crowd of workers, but how many may never be known. Estimates range from anywhere between 600 to 3,000 people huddled in the rain to listen.

Spies spoke, passionately, as always, but not for very long. He spoke for a few minutes to rally the crowd. After him came Albert Parsons, who was from the state of Alabama and the editor of the English-language radical newspaper *The Alarm*. Unlike Spies, Parsons was long-winded. He ended up shouting his rhetoric from the back of that horse cart for over an hour as the rain poured down on the people and speakers. According to newspapers, Parsons was fired up and he gained in strength with each passing minute, his speech becoming more and more radical the longer it went on. Over the years, however, this account has become debatable, at the very least, and likely untrue.

In fact, the crowd and the speakers, according to many, seemed very calm. It was almost boring. Chicago Mayor Carter Harrison, Sr. had stopped by the event to watch. However, the event ended up being so boring and uninteresting to him that he left long before it was over, heading to his home for the night. He thought nothing more about the whole event.

After Parsons had gone on for the better part of two hours, he stepped aside. Anarchist and activist Samuel Fielden stepped up next. His speech was also brief. He spoke for about ten minutes. It was now about 10:30 at night, and as Fielden was wrapping up his speech, more police arrived. Once Fielden was finished, the policemen gathered en masse near one end of the square. They told the gatherers and the speakers that they had to end their rally and disperse. If not, people would be arrested and force could be used.

Police were gathered in a line. They began to march forward, their leader telling the crowd to disperse. What happened next is not in dispute, but who was responsible has remained the mystery for over a century. Someone threw a homemade round bomb with a lighted fuse. The bomb was encased in a light metal shell. The bomb landed near the line of policemen who immediately froze in their tracks. The fuse sputtered and appeared to go out for a moment, and then exploded in a hail of fire, smoke, and shrapnel. Policeman Mathias J. Degan was sprayed with shrapnel and went down immediately. Other police were hit with the deadly metal and the air was filled with the sound of policemen and the crowd screaming. Police began to fire into the crowd.

The debate still rages, to this very day, over who fired first. Newspapers, such as *The New York Times*, said that the demonstrators opened fire on police first. Others refuted that. Whoever fired first, it is known that both sides exchanged fire. Now bullets rang off of the walls of buildings and the stone street. More screams filled the air and soon people ran in every direction, trying to run away from Haymarket Square.

One of the police officers, an Inspector Bonfield, shouted for a cease-fire. He became worried that with all of the smoke and darkness, they might accidentally fire on each other. In fact, in the coming days, weeks, months, and years, there would be many who agreed that a lot of the police casualties were likely inflicted by friendly fire, as confused policemen fired at anything that moved. And considering the confusion and smoke, they likely shot at each other.

When it was all over, there were about sixty police officers wounded. As far as the civilians, it may never be known how many were wounded, since so many fled and then feared arrest if they sought treatment. There were seven dead policemen and about four dead workers. One policeman would eventually die two years later from complications stemming from wounds he received that night.

The city was outraged. The newspapers inflamed the public, and many of them published inaccurate numbers. Some claimed that as many as fifty people lay on the ground dead. Others inflated the number of police that were killed. Papers that were against the workers, and anarchists in particular, ended up with the loudest voices, and they demanded that anyone who had anything to do with the rally be rounded up, arrested, and held responsible for the deaths of the police officers. Some contended that whether or not the speakers involved threw the bombs or fired on the police, they were there inciting this and had, in effect, condoned the violence and should be brought up on charges.

The police reacted to the hysteria by completely throwing out whatever rights suspects had. They raided homes in Bohemian and German neighborhoods. They tore apart homes and apartments looking for bomb-making equipment and suspect literature. In their haste, they did not get search warrants, something required even at that time. Numerous people were arrested and then re-arrested, questioned, and released. Police, and then the press at the time, put the blame squarely on the shoulders of the anarchists and demonstration organizers. It was said that the entire event had been planned as a kind of trap to lure in police so that the bomb could be thrown and officers killed. Much of the public, at the time, believed that this was the case and the cries for revenge and blood-for-blood rang out loud and clear.

The police went into a kind of hysteria. They raided the offices of *Arbeiter-Zeitung*. They arrested the editor, August Spies, as well as his brother, an editorial assistant and editor named Michael Schwab, and a typesetter named Adolph Fischer. Spies' brother was not charged and later released. The police then searched the premises, where a copy of the original flier, asking the workers to show up armed, was found. They also found other evidence that the prosecutors felt was incriminating.

On May 7, police staged another raid. This one was on the residence of a man named Louis Lingg. There they discovered a host of bomb-making equipment and partially made bombs. Then police tracked down a man named Balthazar Rau, who was suspected of being the bomber in the city of Omaha. He was brought back to Chicago and also charged. He offered to give evidence against others he claimed were in on the plot. He stated that the defendants had been experimenting with explosives and dynamite. He also claimed that they had published a special code

114

word in the most recent issue of *Arbeiter-Zeitung,* which was supposed to signify that the workers were to show up armed. He claimed that word was "ruhe," which translated to "peace."

A trial was soon to begin, and to many in the modern world, it was a travesty of justice. Several speakers who were there that night did not get caught in the initial police round-up. However, several of them felt that the evidence against those arrested was so weak that they turned themselves in. Among those was Albert Parsons. Another member who was rounded up and arrested, an assistant editor at Spies' newspaper, Michael Schwab, had not even been at Haymarket Square, but had spoken at a different rally that was being held at the same time. In the rush to arrest as many avowed anarchists for the crime, they ended up getting a few that had nothing to do with the incident.

The trial, known as Illinois vs. Spies et al, began on June 21, 1886. The trial would go on until August 11 that same year. The presiding judge was Joseph Gary, who was vehemently and obviously against the defendants and their cause. He was openly hostile to them whenever they brought a motion before him. Throughout the course of the trial, he would rule in favor of the prosecution. He also let much of the trial degenerate into hostility and chaos. It became a trial about the belief of anarchists in general; the actual truth of what happened that night got lost in the noise raised by prosecutors and a media eager to sell papers and fan the flames of hysteria.

The selection of the jury itself took three weeks. The defendants' lawyers found themselves continually harassed. Nearly a thousand men were called to be potential jurors. After three weeks, when the twelve jurors were seated, most of them had declared in open court that they bore prejudice against the defendants. Anyone who claimed any sympathy towards unions or the cause of the workers was dismissed by the prosecution. Meanwhile, the defense had burned through their allotted challenges and had to settle for what they had.

When the trial began, the list of people who testified against the defendants was huge. By the time the trial was over, the jury had listened to 118 people. Of those, 54 members of the Chicago Police Department also testified. All of the defendants also took the stand in their own defense.

It was the prosecution's contention that all of the defendants were guilty of conspiracy. They argued that even if they had not actually thrown the bomb themselves, they also did nothing to stop it. Furthermore, they argued, they had so riled up the crowd with their rhetoric, that they had actively encouraged the violence that erupted that night.

As the trial went on, what constituted a conspiracy seemed to expand to nearly anything and everything that might have pointed to the defendants ever having spoken, even in passing, about the use of violence to meet their goals. The prosecution even argued that any attempts for the demonstrators to defend against the police constituted a conspiracy to commit violence. One of the policemen who had a piece of shrapnel removed from his chest had that piece of shrapnel chemically analyzed by scientists. Those scientists testified that the metal in that bomb was chemically identical to the explosives that had been found in Lingg's home. It was testified that the anarchists had apparently been experimenting with dynamite and other forms of explosives and bomb designs until they had come up with the version that had been used that night.

When both sides rested and the jury left the courtroom, it was discovered that instructions on whether or not to find the defendants guilty of manslaughter had not been given. The entire jury was called back into the courtroom and those instructions were read. It turned out not to have made much of a difference, however. The jury found all eight defendants guilty.

At the sentencing, several of the defendants spoke. Several of them accused the police of being far worse instigators and gangs than the defendants had been. They were then read their fates. Seven of the defendants were sentenced to death by hanging and a man named Oscar Neebe was sentenced to 15 years in prison.

The verdict caused an outcry around the world from workers' groups. Protests were held around the globe demanding that a just verdict be handed down for the defendants. The trial, even at the time, was called a travesty.

The case was appealed. The Illinois Supreme Court unanimously confirmed the verdicts and sentences. The U.S. Supreme Court then had their chance. The petition for certiorari was denied.

Once the appeals had been exhausted, pleas to politicians who might be able to do something about the sentencing were looked into. Illinois Governor Richard James Oglesby commuted two of the death sentences to life in prison. Then, Lingg committed suicide the night before his execution. He reportedly used a smuggled dynamite cap to do the duty, holding the dynamite in his mouth like a cigar. The explosion blew off half his face and he died in agony over the next six hours.

The executions were carried out on November 11, 1887. Spies, Parsons, Fischer, and Engel were led to the gallows wearing white robes and hoods over their heads. On the way to the gallows, the men sang. They sang "La Marseillaise" and then an anthem for the international revolutionary movement. Family members of Lucy Parsons, wife of the soon-to-be-executed Parsons, were detained and searched for bombs. Before Spies was hanged with the others, he stepped forward and spoke.

> The time will come when our silence will be more powerful than the voices you strangle today!

The men dropped. The nooses did not break their necks. They slowly strangled at the end of the ropes, leaving many witnesses shaken.

It all sounds cut and dry, correct? To many, it was. However, over the years, the facts have been studied again and again. In fact, the true identity of the bomber was never revealed. The men who were convicted were not identified, even by police, as the people who actually threw the bomb. Instead, they were convicted of conspiracy to commit the act.

Thus, the mystery remains, who threw the bomb? For many who have studied the case, the most likely suspect is Schnaubelt, the man who was arrested twice and then fled the country. In fact, in subsequent years, he was reportedly identified as a provocateur, and not a real anarchist. Many say he was planted and told to throw the bomb by forces against the workers' movement, so the police would have a reason to make the arrests that they made and to hang the people they hanged. Other suspects have been named by many authors and researchers over the years. However, no one was ever really convicted of throwing the actual bomb that killed and injured those policemen that night.

The tide had turned against worker's thanks to the media's portrayal of those who were on trial as cold-blooded monsters. The cause of the eight-hour workday was set back by several years. However, it did come back, as did unions, and many reforms were made to protect workers and to keep them safe.

In Chicago, memorials were erected for those involved in the riot. At first, a statue was put up to memorialize the policemen who were killed or wounded. Then, after years of protests and continued evidence that the people convicted and hanged had nothing to do with the incident, a memorial was erected in their honor, as well.

As for who was really responsible for the violence that night, the world will likely never know for sure. It remains yet another enduring Chicago mystery.

Chapter Seventeen
The Unsolved Murders of John Wayne Gacy

These days, there are fewer names that bring about a look of terror more than John Wayne Gacy. He was, for a time, the most prolific serial killer that the U.S. had ever seen. The horror that was Gacy still manages to shock people when they look at his case. How did a man manage to appear to much of the world as a respectable businessman—a man who even dressed as a clown for children's parties—manage to murder so many young men and boys. And how, and why, did he bury so many of them in the crawlspace of his home? How did he get away with it for so long? And, the biggest question, were there more murders than the 33 he was ultimately convicted and executed for?

The life of John Wayne Gacy started out normal, like nearly everyone else's. He was born in March of 1942, the second of three children to John Stanley Gacy and his wife, Marion, in the city of Chicago. He was of Polish and Danish persuasion, but he was always unathletic and overweight, even as a child, which made him a bit of an outcast among his friends and schoolmates. Gacy grew up close to his two sisters and his mother, but his father was alcoholic and he and John Wayne found themselves unable to get along well. His father was also physically abusive to the younger John.

For the young Gacy, his relationship with his father would define much of his younger years. He strove to win his father's approval on anything, but seldom found any love or praise. Gacy would later say that one of his earliest memories was being beaten by his father, who used a leather belt on him. His father was also routinely verbally abusive to the young Gacy, putting him down and making fun of him. When things got worse between the young Gacy and his father, and after one particularly vicious beating with a belt, his mother attempted to get between him and his father, and was not entirely successful. Then, to make matters worse and spur Gacy on toward the path that would lead him to serial murder, he was molested at the age of nine by a family friend.

Gacy underwent repeated abuse of physical and verbal varieties for most of his childhood and until he reached the age of 18. At that point, he became involved in politics. He became a standing member of the Democratic Party and worked as a precinct captain in his neighborhood.

If he was seeking approval in this matter from his father, he did not receive it. Gacy ended up moving around the state of Illinois while being involved in various political offices and elections.

He also had a variety of jobs, including that of a salesman, that moved him around the state. At one time, he had a job as a mortuary attendant and had a room and cot behind the embalming room. From there, he observed the morticians embalming corpses and, at one time, also climbed into a coffin containing the body of a young man, where he lay with it and caressed it before becoming repulsed by his own actions.

After that, Gacy decided to try and at least make his outward appearance appear as normal as possible. He pursued a woman named Marlynn. While he courted her, he also had his first homosexual experience. He became a high-ranking member of the local Jaycees and very active in their activities. Eventually, he married Marlynn.

His father-in-law offered him the chance to manage three Kentucky Fried Chicken restaurants that he had bought in Waterloo, Iowa. This was in 1966, and the salary offered was lucrative at the time at over $15,000 a year, and he would also get a share of the profits from the three restaurants. Gacy was required to complete a relatively easy managerial course and then he and his wife moved to Waterloo, Iowa, where he began to manage the three fast-food chains.

To all the world, John Wayne Gacy and his wife, Marlynn, were the most normal married couple you could want. He appeared to be a very successful businessman and was active in community events with the local Jaycees. He and his wife even helped bring two children into the world. One of them was a son and another a daughter. In 1967, even his father admired what he had accomplished and said that he was wrong about calling Gacy a "sissy" most of his life.

What many did not know is that there was a darker and seedier side of the Jaycees in the Waterloo, Iowa, area. Members often engaged in activities such as wife-swapping, prostitution, pornography, and heavy drug usage. Gacy found nearly all of his dark sexual desires right there and available to him, and he cheerfully and actively engaged in the acts. He regularly cheated on his wife during that time and even supposedly opened a private club in his basement, where underage employees of his restaurants were invited to drink and play pool. He was seen mostly engaging in social activities with the male members of his staff. He then began making sexual advances toward many of his young male workers.

Then in August 1967, Gacy was known to commit his first sexual assault on a teenage boy. The boy's name was Donald Vorhees and he was the son of a fellow Jaycee member. He reportedly, and later admittedly, lured the young man to his home on the pretext of watching porn. He then began giving the young man alcohol and blackmailed the young man into performing oral sex on him. Gacy also managed to convince other young men that he was engaging in some kind of "scientific experiment" that required him to engage in homosexual acts on young men. At times, Gacy was willing to pay the young men who engaged in these acts with him.

Eventually, Vorhees reported to his father that Gacy had been regularly sexually assaulting him. Vorhees' father called the police. Gacy was arrested and charged with sodomy with regards to Vorhees and attempted sexual assault against a 16-year-old boy. Gacy denied the charges and he demanded that he be administered a polygraph. He ended up taking the test, but the test proved that he was lying. Despite even this, Gacy denied that he had done anything wrong. Publicly, Gacy maintained that the charges were politically motivated and had to do with his nomination as president of the Iowa Jaycees. In 1968, Gacy was indicted on the sodomy charge.

Despite his protestations that everything was politically motivated and that he had not done anything wrong, Gacy's attorney advised him to enter a guilty plea on one count of sodomy in the case brought by Vorhees. He continued to plead not guilty to the other molestation charges leveled against him by other young men. An arraignment was held in 1968 and Gacy told the judge that he and Vorhees had engaged in various sexual acts, but that he had participated out of curiosity rather than anything demonic or evil. The judge did not believe him and Gacy was sentenced to ten years in prison. Just after that, his wife filed for divorce and that was granted in September of 1969.

Gacy began serving his sentence at Anamosa State Penitentiary. He was a model prisoner while there. Within months after his arrival, he rose to the rank of head cook in the kitchen. He also continued his work with the Jaycees and joined the group in prison. During this time, he increased the prison membership from 50 to 650. He also reportedly worked on behalf of the rights of the inmates and helped get their pay increased for those working in the mess hall. He even oversaw construction of a miniature golf course in the prison recreation yard.

In June of 1969, he petitioned the Iowa Parole Board for an early release. He was denied. While preparing for another parole hearing a year later, Gacy completed sixteen high school courses and earned his high school diploma in November of 1969. That same year, on Christmas, his father died of cirrhosis of the liver. Gacy was not told that his father had died until two days after the incident happened, and it was reported that when he was informed, he broke down and had to be supported by two other inmates. He requested a compassion release to visit his family due to his father's death, but that was also denied.

In June of 1970, Gacy was granted the parole he sought. He was to be on parole for twelve months. He had served only eighteen months of his ten-year sentence for the sodomy charges. When he was released, he initially told friends that he wanted to re-establish himself in Waterloo, but then, within twenty-four hours of his release, he packed up and moved back to Chicago with his mother and soon found work as a short-order cook.

Gacy began to rebuild his life. Once again, the *Jekyll and Hyde* nature of Gacy began to take hold. He began to establish himself as a model citizen for all the world to see. He became involved in the Jaycees again, and then set out to start a business. He began a successful contracting and construction business. Involved in local politics, he again raised money and engaged in local Democratic events and party initiatives. It was while in Chicago that he created the character of Pogo the Clown and began entertaining at children's birthday parties and other events. He was so successful that he was given numerous business awards and had his photograph taken with First Lady Rosalynn Carter.

Throughout the 1970s, for all the world knew, Gacy was a model man and businessman. What no one suspected, however, was that Gacy had a very dark side. He had urges that overpowered him, and when that happened, the monster came out. Almost from the time he came back to Chicago, he indulged those dark sides, and he escalated them to include murder.

In January of 1972, Gacy went cruising. He visited the Greyhound bus terminal on Chicago's south side and picked up a 15-year-old boy named Timothy Jack McCoy. Gacy promised the young man that he could spend the night at Gacy's home and get some shelter and that, in the morning, Gacy would give him a ride back to the bus station. Gacy insisted that, during the night, he awoke in the middle of night and found McCoy standing in his bedroom with a knife in his hand.

Gacy stated that he attacked McCoy. McCoy covered his head with his hands in a gesture of surrender, but Gacy pounced anyway, stating he was convinced he was being attacked. He pushed McCoy up against a wall and threw him against a dresser. When the young man fell to the floor, Gacy grabbed the dropped knife and stabbed the young man in the chest repeatedly. Gacy then staggered into the kitchen where he found eggs and a slab of bacon on the counter and two place settings at the table. McCoy, it turned out, had walked into the bedroom to wake Gacy up because he was making breakfast, carrying the knife in his hand absentmindedly. Gacy quickly took McCoy's body and buried it in his crawlspace beneath his house, covering the body with a layer of concrete.

Gacy would tell interviewers about this incident years later after he had been convicted of the murders of 33 young men. He would tell the interviewer that he was completely drained after the incident. At the same time, he said, he had an orgasm while on top of the young man, stabbing him to death. It was his first real taste of blood and he realized that death and murder was the ultimate thrill. The monster was now fully out of its cage, and Gacy's unbridled fury was unleashed upon numerous young men and boys across the Chicago area.

Gacy used a variety of methods to find his victims. He returned, many times, to the Greyhound bus station. As a man who ran a construction business, he also had young men come to him during the summer months looking for work, and he soon began to prey on them. He was often careful to find those who had run away from home, or had problems at home. Their disappearances were often not reported for a very long time, since so many had a reputation of running away.

Gacy buried many of his victims around his home in unincorporated Des Plaines, including in the crawlspace beneath his home. He even buried one body beneath a newly-laid cement floor in his garage. When his crawlspace became too crowded with bodies, he also dumped them in the Des Plaines River, not far from his home.

It was only a matter of time before his crimes would be found. Family members began to file reports of missing men. Gacy had taken so many and from so many areas, it took a long time for police to start piecing things together. Eventually, enough connections were found leading from the missing men back to Gacy that he became the prime suspect. When police entered his home for questioning and smelled a foul odor coming from the vents, they achieved a warrant that allowed them to dig in the man's crawlspace. Gacy was arrested and the horrors that had been going on within his seemingly quiet suburban Chicago home were revealed. The Chicago news was filled with gruesome details of the murders as they were uncovered, night after night and morning after morning. Images of body after body being removed from the home were broadcast. The home was torn apart as the search for bodies continued into the backyard and beyond.

When arrested, at first, Gacy confessed to the murders, but his confession was rambling and nonsensical at times. Gacy was eventually tried and convicted for thirty-three murders. He was sentenced to death, and sent off to Death Row. He remained on Death Row, conducting interviews with the press and engaging in his hobby of painting, until 1994. There were reports that one of the tubes leading into his arm clogged and caused a few problems during his execution, but many felt Gacy still got off quieter and easier than his victims.

For many, Gacy's death was the end, but for other family members, there is still a question. Did Gacy kill more than the thirty-three men he was convicted of killing? Some people, including members of the police force, say that it may have happened.

According to one police officer who investigated the Gacy case, Gacy as much as admitted that there were more bodies. After police pulled body after body out of the man's home, they looked for more near the Des Plaines River, where Gacy indicated he had also disposed of bodies. Police Detective Rafael Tolvar reportedly looked Gacy in the eye and asked, "Where are the rest of them?" According to Tolvar, Gacy looked back and said, "That's for you guys to find out." The same detective said that Gacy even suggested that a number around forty-five might be the right number.

When Gacy was arrested, another police officer said it sparked a memory. He remembered a time when Gacy lived in an apartment complex. At the time, Gacy worked the grounds, tending the bushing, mowing the lawns, and doing some basic gardening. This police detective recalled a time that he was driving down a road, near the apartment complex, early in the morning (about 3 a.m.) and saw Gacy carrying a shovel. Others who also lived in the apartment complex came forward and said they remembered Gacy digging at odd hours, including the middle of the night. He always had a reason or excuse for it, saying that he had work to do and his regular job prevented him from doing it any other time. Other residents, including a woman who lived at the complex with her husband in a garden apartment, said in an interview with police that they would often see Gacy digging in the yard at all hours of the night. He would dig trenches in apparently random patterns rather than in a pattern that would be normal when it came to gardening. She also said that young men were sometimes with him and helped him.

There is another matter of police reports from the time when Gacy was arrested. Reporters and others who have looked at those reports in the subsequent years say that several reports show that, even at the time, police suspected that there might be more bodies buried in and around the apartment complex where Gacy worked as a maintenance man. Most of the bodies, they guessed, were in the grassy part of the front and back lawn, and beneath what is now a parking lot.

The police eventually did show up at the apartment complex with a ground radar. The company that was hired to do the scanning said that they found 17 possible anomalies that they felt might contain bodies. The company insists that police only looked at two spots and when nothing was found, they indicated that there was nothing more to it.

Some have suggested that the police are embarrassed by the possibility that more bodies are buried and have never been found and that they just want to forget it.

To make matters more confusing, over the past couple of years, it has been discovered that at least two men who were thought to have been victims of Gacy were actually alive and well. In both cases, parents had come forward and submitted missing persons reports and investigators guessed that remains that had been found at Gacy's home belonged to the men reported missing. It later turned out that these men had simply run away from home because they wanted to, for various reasons, and had lost contact with their families.

And still, there are families who wonder. They wonder if Gacy's rage at the world that expressed itself in torture and murder of young men continued beyond the humble home in unincorporated Des Plaines, Illinois. They wonder, and they continue to wonder, as the man who would know, Gacy himself, is now long gone.

Chapter Eighteen
Was it Really a Cow?
Or Was it Something,
Or Someone Else?

If you were to walk up to any random person almost anywhere in the world and ask them what started the Great Chicago Fire, almost to a man, that person would probably say the same thing. They would smirk, cock their head, and say, "The cow." Some of the more well-read people might even attach a name to that and say, "Mrs. O'Leary's cow." That's the story that has been handed down for over 100 years now. In fact, at the time it first happened, O'Leary and her cow were held accountable and ended up on trial for the destruction that wiped out what was one of the fastest-growing cities in the country at the time. There's just one little problem with that answer, and it was a problem that the court dealt with even at the time. The fact is, it isn't true. The fact remains, no one knows for sure what caused the Great Chicago Fire, although there do seem to be a few likely suspects, and several of them are more likely than Mrs. O'Leary and her bovine tenant.

Chicago, in 1871, was a disaster waiting to happen. The city had been expanding like a balloon for years. The population explosion had not been handled well by the city planners. People were allowed to build any kind of house they wanted, virtually anywhere. Businesses were built from wood. Houses were built from wood. Even the streets were made from wood planks that were laid down across what otherwise would have been bare dirt. Combining that with the high winds that were common off the lake, and you had a tinderbox, given just the right circumstances.

Those circumstances were just right in 1871. The summer was dry and hot. The city had no electrical method to keep all of the fire stations in communication with one another. Instead, each neighborhood had a fire station call box that would ring at a fire station. The firehouses, meanwhile, had lookout towers and would staff them with a firefighter who would keep watch over the city. If smoke was seen, or flames detected, either a neighbor could use the call box, or the smoke and flames might be spotted by a sharp-eyed firefighter in his tower. It was hardly foolproof, and that summer, the fire departments across the city had been busy.

It was 9 p.m. on a Sunday night, October 8, when one of the greatest disasters in the history of the country began. A small fire was started near or inside a small barn located at 137 DeKoven Street. This was very close to where Mrs. O'Leary and her husband lived. They did indeed have a cow and the story began to spread that the cow kicked over a lantern and that sparked the fire.

Once the fire started a series of events, including a number of serious mistakes made by the exhausted firefighters, ended up making what should have been an easy crisis into a full-blown disaster that would take much of the Windy City with it.

The firefighters in the neighborhood where the fire started were tired. There had been numerous fires throughout the week. In fact, just the night before they had been out battling a particularly destructive and nasty fire. They were hoping to get some rest. Little did they know that the city was at its maximum point for destruction. The wood that made up the buildings, houses, sidewalks, and streets was particularly dry. Rain had not been in the forecast for some time. The winds were high, especially that night. The winds were blowing strong from the southwest, sure to carry the sparks from any fire into other buildings that was also just waiting to burst into flames.

The fire was spotted by a neighbor that night. The neighbor ran to a nearby pharmacy and called the fire station using the call box. The firefighters were told, however, that the fire was small. When the neighbor got back, he discovered that the fire had already spread and had started a second fire nearby. He then ran back to the call box, but, in his haste and panic, he gave the firefighters the wrong directions, sending them in the opposite direction from where the fire actually was. The first call came into the fire station at 9:40 p.m.

A second problem began to form. When the dry wood caught fire, the wood exploded. The fire was so hot that it began to generate its own wind. This is something that firefighters are familiar with, and especially those who battle forest fires. The flames themselves, essentially, create their own wind and that further fans the flames. As the sparks from the original fire, carried into the air by the strong southwest winds, touched upon the dry wood of other homes and buildings, the wood caught fire immediately. The more structures that caught fire, the more wind the fire itself generated. The natural southwest wind combined with the wind generated by the fire created a kind of hurricane of fire.

Residents were awakened by the flames. They began to try and fight the fire, but there was not enough water to help and there was nothing that they could do to battle the winds. The air itself seemed on fire and the night was filled with sparks and burning debris. Each spark and piece of debris started another fire. Residents began to run and they ran for

the Chicago River, which bisected the downtown area. The southwest winds were also pushing the fire in that direction, but residents would find that there was no rescue or respite for them at the river's edge.

The problem was that the edge of the Chicago River was crowded with boats. Those boats were often made of wood and contained wood because the banks of the river were lined with piles of coal, as well as lumber yards. In that sense, the Chicago River was the worst place for people to flee to, as it was already packed, end to end, with fuel for the flames. Plus, the super-heated air that was being pushed ahead of the flames, fanned by the tremendous wind, was causing rooftops to burst into flames well ahead of the fire itself. So, residents fleeing into the streets (which were made of wood) or on sidewalks (also made of wood) found themselves in air and wind that was so hot, it was like being inside an oven. All around them, homes and buildings were exploding into flame and even the hoped-for respite of water at the Chicago River could do nothing to hold the flames at bay. When a church at the edge of the river caught fire, the flames leapt into the air and sent debris into the wood and coal at the edge; the wind lifted sparks and embers into the air from that and soon the flames had crossed the edge of the river. Now, ahead of it, was the main business district of Chicago, plus dozens of mansions and wealthy homes. None of them stood a chance before the wall of fire.

All around the city, attempts were made to put out the fire. They all met with disaster. No one could stand up to the onslaught. Once again, the wind was the enemy. As soon as one fire was brought under control, the wind would carry embers and debris to the next home. It was a lost cause and the residents, now a mix of the poorest in the city and the wealthiest, grabbed what they could and headed for places they thought might be safe.

Residents ran for the open spaces of Lincoln Park and to the shores of Lake Michigan. As they stood there, bathed in the firelight, they looked back to see the city that had been their home burn to the ground. Some of the finest examples of early architecture were destroyed. Grand hotels and office buildings were scorched and then burned. Nearly everything that had been Chicago was gone. Even Chicago's City Hall did not survive.

When the fire was over, the mayor placed the city under martial law. There was a regiment of the Union Army in the city at the time, headed by a man named Philip Sheridan. The mayor issued a proclamation that Sheridan was now in charge of the city. To his credit, Sheridan did not abuse his power, but handled relief efforts, and he found that most of the residents were willing to work with him. Martial law was lifted after just a few days. Sheridan had a home in Chicago, which was

Was it Really a Cow? Or Was it Something , Or Someone Else?

miraculously spared, but he lost all of his personal and professional papers and documents in the fire.

The fire itself continued to burn for about a day. On Monday night, it began to rain. The winds began to die down. When it was over, the fire had burned a path straight through the heart of Chicago and completely destroyed roughly thirty-four city blocks.

Hundreds of people were dead. In truth, the death toll for the tragedy was much less than many expected. A vast majority of the population of the city was able to get out of their homes and get to safety. However, the property damage was almost unimaginable. The city had a population around 300,000 and about 90,000 people were now homeless. The property damage was somewhere around $222 million.

People wanted to know how this had happened. It is true that the origin of the fire was the O'Leary barn. With the way the winds were blowing, the irony of the situation was that the O'Leary home was spared. Sparks and embers blew away from their house, leaving their home relatively unscathed.

It was a newspaper story that first came up with the tale of the Mrs. O'Leary and her cow. A reporter named Michael Ahern, working for *The Chicago Tribune* stated that O'Leary had gone into the barn to milk her cow using a lantern to help her see. The cow had been restless and kicked over the lantern, which landed in a pile of straw. The flames then caught the barn on fire and the rest, as they say, was history. The story immediately caught the public's attention. Ahern later retracted his story, saying he made it up because he thought it made for good copy and an interesting tale, but that it was entirely concocted. It was too late for the O'Leary family, however, as the story had already become embedded in the minds of the general public and no amount of retraction by the press could stop the story from spreading or sticking.

O'Leary was the perfect scapegoat for the time. She was an Irish immigrant. The Irish were flocking to the United States at the time after famine and other problems in their home country made living there untenable for most. She was also a Catholic, which was not a popular thing in the Chicago area at the time (although that has certainly changed over the years). Irish Catholics were a minority in the country and, generally, discriminated against and despised, whether they deserved it or not. Even before all of the fires were out, the story had caught on and people chose to believe it.

O'Leary was even brought into court to defend herself. Ultimately, she denied the fire had been started in the barn when she was milking her cow. She claimed she had been inside, with her husband, when the barn caught fire. She was actually exonerated by the court. That still did not change the story in the minds of the general populace. In fact, to this day, it is generally thought that O'Leary's cow started the fire.

Well, if the cow and Mrs. O'Leary were blameless, who *did* start the fire? There are a couple of suspects that seem like they might be better candidates than an innocent woman persecuted because of her nationality, religion, and an innocent barn animal.

At least one historian believes that the man who started the fire was named Daniel "Pegleg" Sullivan. He was the man who first reported the fire. The theory is that he had snuck into the barn to try and steal milk, lit a lantern, and then knocked the lantern over himself when trying to make his getaway. He may have even had an accomplice in the form of a neighbor of O'Leary named Dennis Regan.

Regan testified that he also called authorities about the fire when he was in his home. He lived at 112 De Koven Street, right nearby. He claimed that he saw flames engulfing the barn and immediately called the fire department. He also said he heard someone outside the barn yelling for help. He claimed to have attempted to warn the O'Learys and tried to put out the fire himself.

The problem is that his story is full of holes. The most egregious of the claims is that he saw the fire when, in fact, if you were to stand at his home and look in the direction of the barn you would have been completely unable to see the O'Leary barn. Also, there was a party going on not far from the O'Leary home and none of the party-goers claimed to have heard the shouting that Regan said he heard and that brought him over to the O'Leary home.

The theory is that Regan and Sullivan were in cahoots in trying to steal some milk from the O'Learys. When they accidentally started the fire, they concocted the story to try to cover up their involvement.

Another possible suspect, suggested by a relatively recent *Chicago Tribune* writer, is that a man named Louis M. Cohn might have had something to do with the fire. Cohn would go on to become a newspaper man himself in his later days. At the time of the fire, however, he was a teenager. He and his friends, the story goes, were in the barn playing a game of craps. When the noise they were making awoke Mrs. O'Leary, she came out to the barn to see what was going on. Cohn and his friends immediately panicked and tried to run away, but one of them kicked over a lantern which caught the straw on fire and set the blaze. According to the recent *Chicago Tribune* article, Cohn even reportedly confessed to the fire in his will.

Then, of course, there are the people who think that a single person was not responsible, in the least, for the catastrophe. That same day, as Chicago burned, there were other fires in and around the region and many of them were much worse in terms of population deaths than

Chicago. In fact, there were four large fires all around the shores of Lake Michigan that same day.

The next theory was first suggested back in 1882 and then looked at again in the 20th Century: The fire was possibly started by a meteor shower. Some say that Biela's Comet broke up over the Midwest, causing parts of itself to rain down on Chicago and much of the Lake Michigan region. That would explain, goes the theory, why fires in the city of Peshtigo in Northeastern Wisconsin, and on the shores of Lake Michigan, started at almost exactly the same time as the Great Chicago Fire.

The theory, according to scientists, does not hold up. It has been proven that meteorites that hit the earth are not hot, like they were initially thought. Often the rocks are cool to the touch just minutes after they hit the earth. As such, scientists say, there was no way for meteorites to start any of the fires that day.

As for Sullivan and Cohn, they were never charged and no one ever tried them in a court of law or presented evidence of their involvement in the fire.

As such, we may never truly know who started the Great Chicago Fire or how. That's probably the biggest reason why most people still think that a woman who was just trying to milk her cow ended up sparking one of the most famous disasters in the history of America.

Part Four
The Bizarre

And now we come to the strangest part of the book. Although this is probably the shortest of the sections, the two stories presented here are certainly the strangest. As odd as it is to have residents who have seemingly vanished into thin air, and respectable residents burying dozens of bodies beneath their homes, or the theory that a comet caused the fire that nearly destroyed Chicago for all time, nothing compares to the two stories left in this book.

It may be the fact that these are so strange that they have not been solved. In both cases, the culprits of the events discussed here have never been found. And, for many, the incidents that they inspired have left people discussing them for decades, laughing strangely, shaking their heads and then wondering who could have done it. The answers remain elusive.

In at least one case, the first that we shall discuss in this section, a huge manhunt was launched at the time. Despite this, the culprit turned out to be insanely clever to the point that they were able to outwit and outlast the federal government agents sent to track them down. As for the second story, well, the manhunt has not been quite so extensive and the incidents go beyond the borders of Chicago into other cities, as well.

So, be prepared to enter the world of the truly strange. Here are two unsolved mysteries that just seem to defy any other classification than "bizarre."

Chapter Nineteen
The Max Headroom
Pirate Broadcast of 1987

It is hard to imagine this incident. Take a moment and close your eyes and imagine that it is late on a Sunday night. The weekend is nearly over and you are already mentally preparing for the start of the work week. It is about 9 p.m. in Chicago. Outside, the air is turning cold and it has gotten dark at about 6 p.m. for a few weeks now. Winter is fast approaching, and the Thanksgiving holiday is just days away. There is anticipation for the holidays, but you still have to get ready for work. The popular local television station WGN broadcasts the local news at 9 p.m. Perhaps you turn into that broadcast to catch up on the day's news, sports, and weather. Or, maybe, as a sci-fi fan you have turned over the WTTW, the local PBS station, to watch an episode of *Doctor Who*. Suddenly, just as you are getting into either of those shows, the screen goes all snowy and fuzzy. Then, to your amazed eyes, a strange broadcast starts. The audio is distorted and a bizarre scene of a man wearing a rubber mask and making obscene gestures at the camera completely takes over the broadcast for about a minute and a half. Then, just as suddenly, the broadcast ends and you are back watching the news or the sci-fi show.

For viewers of WGN and WTTW on the night of November 22, 1987, this is exactly what happened. For the FCC and those involved in the broadcast industry, it is known as a "broadcast signal intrusion." For the average viewer, it was a pirate broadcast that overrode the signal for both stations for a time and some pranksters with a twisted and strange sense of humor broadcast their own images for about 90 seconds. It left many puzzled. When the story was later revealed, it provoked both outrage and laughter. It also launched a huge investigation by the FCC and local Chicago police. Finally, it remains unsolved and many still wonder who was behind the Max Headroom Pirate Broadcast of 1987.

Before we can look at this incident, a few things need to be explained. Since this happened in 1987, just enough things have changed in the world and the city of Chicago to make people wonder what is being discussed. The world of 1987 was very different than it is today, at least as far as broadcasting is concerned. Although cable television was growing in popularity, not everyone in the Chicago area had it. Most people still caught the television signal broadcast from towers located downtown, using antennas on top of the house or hooked up to the televisions themselves.

Downtown Chicago was a conglomeration of tall buildings, but there were three that dominated the skyline at the time. If you were looking at downtown from the west, facing Lake Michigan, the tall building on the far left, looking like a kind of elongated trapezoid, was the John Hancock Center. Topping the huge building are two gigantic white and red antennas. In the middle was the white tower, today known as Aon Center, but then known as the Standard Oil Building. At the far right was the dark, block building that held the title of "Tallest Building in the World" known as the Sears Tower. Atop that building, as well, are two huge white antenna structures.

Most of the major stations that broadcast to the Chicago area had space on the antennas located on top of the John Hancock Center and the Sears Tower. And, particularly crowded, were the two antennas on top of the Sears Tower. If you had a broadcast facility, how could you not want space on top of the antennas that capped the tallest building in the world? It would give you signal coverage to the entire area, plus potential coverage into Indiana and other neighboring areas.

At that time, the local station WGN (which stood for *World's Greatest Newspaper*, as it was owned by the *Chicago Tribune*) and PBS station WTTW shared space on the antennas on top of the Sears Tower. Their respective antennas were actually very close to one another on the structures. WGN, in particular, was a broadcasting powerhouse, with both a radio station and one of the most popular television stations in the city.

You also need to know who Max Headroom was. In 1987, the idea of computer-generated people being used as television personalities was beginning to catch hold. Max Headroom got his start as a host of a music video show on Channel 4 in Great Britain. Actually, Max was actor Matt Frewer dressed in prosthetics and wearing a plastic suit. The computer-graphic software at that time was not actually able to create a realistic 3D human head that would articulate the way Max was supposed to. So, Frewer would spend hours being made up to look as if he were computer-generated. He would film in front of a blank screen, reading his lines, and then his image would be placed over a hand-drawn background of strange moving lines, and then it would be digitally manipulated to give Max his stutter and strange verbal inflections.

He became a huge hit in Great Britain. He was then made the star of his own television series and brought across the pond to the United States. His show was shown, for a brief time, in the U.S., but he became most famous as a product pitchman for Coca-Cola. He also starred in a popular music video at the time. In 1987, Max Headroom was still popular and ever-present on commercials, television shows, music videos, and countless merchandise that bore his likeness.

On the night of November 22nd of that year, something happened. Somehow, someone, somewhere in the city was able to completely override the signals of both stations. Doing so would have required

133

equipment that was not sold at the local electronics store and some real brains. Despite being smart enough to put that together and get away with it, the people who overrode the signals that night did not have a political agenda, it seems. Instead, they bombarded homes with vulgar images, cursing, and partial nudity.

It began at WGN. The station appears to have been the intended target of the intrusion from the start, judging by some of the things the intruder said during their ninety-second broadcast. The difference between WGN and WTTW was that WGN was broadcasting a live newscast at the time. That meant that there were producers and engineers on site and working when the attempted intrusion happened. Over at WTTW, however, they were broadcasting a pre-recorded show. Their studios were dark, their broadcasting day left to computers and automated systems. Thus, when the intrusion occurred there, it was a much longer process to try and get the signal removed.

The 9 o'clock news broadcast was in full swing on WGN. In fact, it was time for the sports portion of the broadcast. Dan Roan, the sports anchor for the station, was in the middle of doing Chicago Bears football highlights when the strangeness started. Suddenly, the signal turned snowy and static blasted on TVs across the city. Then, the image of a man standing in front of weird moving lines, wearing a suit, and a Max Headroom mask suddenly appeared on their televisions. There was no audio, just a horrendous buzzing sound. It lasted just a few seconds and an engineer flipped a switch that changed the frequency of the WGN studio link to a transmitter located at the John Hancock Building.

The newscast immediately came back on, featuring puzzled and confused anchors. Sports anchor Roan looked particularly flustered. He looked into the camera and said, "Well, if you're wondering what happened, so am I."

The second intrusion actually happened later in the night. WTTW broadcasts old shows of the popular British sci-fi series *Doctor Who* late at night. The entire process was automated, thus eliminating the need for there to be live people at the transmitter or for engineers to be present when shows were broadcast from the station.

At about 11:15 p.m., something bizarre happened. While watching the *Doctor Who* episode known as "Horror of Fang Rock," the signal became fuzzy. This time, it seems, the intruders were able to boost their signal. The image was a bit clearer. The audio was fuzzy and accompanied by a horrendous buzzing sound, but many of the words were clear. What happened next was ninety seconds of outright weirdness that many, even fans of the bizarre sci-fi antics of *Doctor Who* were unable to believe.

The broadcast went something like this:

The screen became fuzzy and full of snow.

The image of a man wearing a brown suit-coat and a rubber Max Headroom mask appeared. Behind him a piece of corrugated metal is waving back and forth, moving up and down in an approximation of the strange moving lines seen behind Max Headroom.

The Max Headroom character speaks in a highly-distorted voice, "He's a freakin' nerd!"

"This guy's better than Chuck Swirsky (another WGN sportscaster). Frickin' Liberal!"

The man bends over to pick something up from the floor.

"Oh, Jesus!"

Picks up a can of Pepsi and holds it up to the camera.

"Catch the wave!"

Throws the can at the camera.

Stares into the camera and begins to bounce and hum the theme to the cartoon "Clutch Cargo." At one point, he walks toward the camera wearing some kind of rubber extension on his middle finger, which is held obscenely for the camera.

"Your love is fading!"

Hums the theme for a few more seconds.

"I stole CBS."

Says something else unintelligible.

"Oh, I just made a giant masterpiece for all of the greatest world newspaper nerds!"

Leans down laughing and making strange noises and comes up with a glove that appears to be a gardening glove.

"My brother has the other one."

He puts the glove partially on one hand.

"It's dirty!"

He throws the glove away.

Suddenly there is more static and the scene switches. The Max Headroom mask is now being held in the man's hand toward the camera. The rubber finger extension is in the mask's mouth. The head of the person cannot be seen as he is bent over, with his pants down and his bare buttocks facing another person standing behind him. Viewers can only see the torso and one hand of the person behind him, but that person is in some kind of dress and holding a flyswatter. The person with the swatter begins to spank the bare buttocks of the person in the brown suit coat.

"They're coming to get me!"

The spanking continues for a few seconds as the mask is held before the camera and the person being spanked yells incoherently for a few more seconds.

The screen goes black and then the episode of *Doctor Who* resumes where it left off.

Fans of the sci-fi show were baffled and confused. Some of them called WTTW. The station, meanwhile was trying to figure out exactly what had happened and who had done it. Angry fans of the television show called the station, flooding the switchboard. Many who were taping the show would not see the bizarre incident until the following day. Of course, interrupting the broadcast of any legal television or radio station is illegal, and falls under the jurisdiction of the Federal Communication Commission (FCC). If the person responsible for the intrusion were caught, it would have resulted in heavy fines and jail time. Thus, the FCC was called and one of the largest manhunts in the history of the organization was launched to try to find the intruder.

Several questions were evident. First, *why* would anyone want to do this? It seemed, judging from the content of the illegal broadcast, that someone had something against WGN. Perhaps it was a disgruntled former employee? Given the technological know-how involved in pulling this off, could it have been a former engineer? The second was, *who* had done this? Again, the possibilities seemed, at first, as if there was quite a narrow pool of people to choose from.

It was theorized that the pirate had overridden the signal for WGN and WTTW using a broadcasting rig at their home or apartment. The signal would have had to have been very strong, bombarding the signal for WTTW as it came off of the antenna located on top of the Sears Tower. To do that would have taken a large amount of equipment. Some felt that a rig capable of this could be bought for about $25,000. Others said that a rig like this could be rented for a few thousand dollars. Still, whatever rig was used, it was not something that could easily be purchased at the corner store. Again, it seemed as if the culprit would be able to be easily tracked down and apprehended.

Another theory was that the person, to be able to do this, had to be relatively close to the Sears Tower. Perhaps an apartment or office building nearly adjacent to the mammoth tower. Again, searches turned up nothing. The pirate had covered his tracks very well, disappearing into the night as mysteriously as he had emerged. Even with the FBI helping with the investigation, no one was found or questioned about the incident.

The reasons why anyone would do this also remain a mystery. No demands were made to WGN or WTTW. No other signal intrusions were noted in and around the date of this one. If the person had a grudge against either station, it would seem that the potential penalties that could have been assessed against him or her outweighed whatever feelings of revenge they might have gotten. The minimum fine for an intrusion like this one was $100,000 and a year in prison was likely.

The Bizarre

Some have suggested that it was just pranksters, perhaps technology geeks who wanted to see if they could do it just for the sake of doing it. This seems the most likely scenario. Considering the events were not repeated, it seems that the pranksters decided that the publicity and potential punishment was too great to attempt committing any more pranks.

As for the television stations, steps were made so that doing such a thing again would be much harder. WTTW improved security around their antenna and signal and also set up a redundant signal at another tower so that the broadcast could easily be switched as was done with WGN earlier that night.

As for the prankster or pranksters that night, no one has ever been arrested or charged over the bizarre incident. These days recordings of the pirate broadcast can be found online on sites such as YouTube. As to who pulled off the prank, the FBI and FCC would still like to know, but it remains yet another Chicago mystery.

Chapter Twenty
The Toynbee Tiles Mystery

Truth be told, this mysterious phenomenon did not actually start in the Chicago area. In fact, the first of the strange objects, now known as Toynbee Tiles, began appearing on streets in and around Philadelphia back in 1983. Then, the phenomenon began to spread. Baltimore, for example, ran an article in their city's newspaper in 1994 about the appearance of these strange signs impressed into the streets. Since that time, copycats have been found in Kansas City, Boston, Washington, D.C., San Francisco, Roswell, New Mexico, Buffalo, Pittsburgh, St. Louis, Cincinnati, Cleveland, and, of course, Chicago. Despite the fact that so many of these tiles have appeared in so many places, even expanding to around the world and showing up in South America, no one knows who is placing them or what the bizarre messages on them mean.

A Toynbee tile is a message apparently created using some kind of tile material, pressed into the asphalt on busy streets around the cities mentioned prior. The exact way in which the tiles are pressed into the pavement itself is also a mystery. Some believe that they are placed on the road covered with something that looks like asphalt and that the passage of cars over the tile eventually presses the white-background message into the softer asphalt and wears away the covering. Whatever the method, once it is placed, the message appears usually as a white background that is embedded into the road itself. What do these tiles say? Well, in the city of Philadelphia there is a wide array of messages, all of them strange. The copycat tiles, including the ones in Chicago, all contain some variation of the following message:

TOYNBEE IDEA
IN KUBRICK'S 2001
RESURRECT DEAD
ON PLANET JUPITER

Strange, huh? What is even stranger is the fact that no one has ever been seen by people or the police installing the tiles. No one is sure of the method of placement or even 100% certain regarding the materials used with the tiles. And, although there are guesses about what the message means, even that is so strange and cryptic that no one knows for sure.

As for what the message means, there have been several attempts to try and decode it. One possibility is that it refers to Arnold Toynbee, a British historian. As for his supposed "idea" referred to within the tiles, some have suggested that it comes from his book *Experiences*, which states:

Human nature presents human minds with a puzzle which they have not yet solved and may never succeed in solving, for all that we can tell. The dichotomy of a human being into "soul" and "body" is not a datum of experience. No one has ever been, or ever met, a living human soul without a body... Someone who accepts—as I myself do, taking it on trust—the present-day scientific account of the Universe may find it impossible to believe that a living creature, once dead, can come to life again; but, if he did entertain this belief, he would be thinking more "scientifically" if he thought in the Christian terms of a psychosomatic resurrection than if he thought in the shamanistic terms of a disembodied spirit.

Another possibility is that the Toynbee reference refers to a Ray Bradbury science-fiction story known as "The Toynbee Convector." That story also refers to a theory by Arnold Toynbee that humankind, in order to survive, must always be advancing and rushing forward to meet the future head-on. And that human beings, also to survive, must always believe in a better future and a better world and that, to do that, humans must think beyond what is possible and into the impossible to achieve that better idea. All in all, that's pretty heady stuff for a tile pressed into asphalt.

As for the Kurbick statement, that obviously refers to Kubrick's seminal science-fiction film *2001: A Space Odyssey*. The movie deals with space travel and the very creation of humankind, perhaps from an alien race. In the movie, a bizarre black monolith is buried beneath the surface of the moon, showing that humans are not the sole living things in the universe. It is then discovered that another, gigantic, monolith is floating around Jupiter. Once space travelers are sent there, one of the astronauts is absorbed into the giant monolith and becomes a being composed almost entirely of energy, raising humans to the next level. As such, some believe that this message is some kind of encouragement that man should try to colonize the moons around Jupiter. Another possibility is referred to in a play by David Mamet where a character explains that "2001" was inspired by Toynbee's theories and that there is a plan in the works to reconstitute life on the planet Jupiter.

Of course, these are all guesses and theories. The tiles that showed up in Chicago were of the kind mentioned above. In Philadelphia, however, there have been other tiles that have gone on to try and explain more of the strange meanings behind the original tiles. One of the largest placements was a series of four tiles placed together, creating a long, rambling, nearly-incoherent tale involving strange government conspiracies, anti-semitic ranting, and blaming media mogul John Knight Ridder for being part of the conspiracy. The four tiles state the following (with some areas illegible):

John Knight Ridder is the Philadelphia thug hellion Jew who'd hated this movements guts—for years—takes money from the Mafia to make the Mafia look good in his newspapers so he has the Mafia in his back pocket. John Knight sent the Mafia to murder me in May 1991 [illegible] journalists [illegible] then gloated to my face about death and Knight Ridder great power to destroy. In fact John Knight went into hellion binge of joy over Knight-Ridder's great power to destroy.

139

I secured house with blast doors and fled the country in June 1991.

NBC attorneys journalists and security officials at Rockefeller Center fraudulently under the 'Freedom of Information Act all [illegible] orders NBC executives got the U.S. federal district attorney's office who got FBI to get Interpol to establish task force that located me in Dover England.

Which back home Inquirer got union goons from their own employees union to [illegible] down a "sports journalist." Who with ease bashed in lights and windows of neighborhood car — as well as men outside my house. They are stationed there still waiting for me.

NBC CBS group "W" Westinghouse, *Time*, Time Warner, Fox, Universal all of the "Cult of the Hellion" each one were Much worse than Knight-Ridder ever was[,] mostly hellion Jews.

When KYW and NBC executives told John Knight the whole coven gloated in joyous fits on how their Soviet pals found a way to turn it into a...

As to what any of that means, there really has been no explanation. Perhaps the tiles are some kind of art exhibit. Or, perhaps, it is someone with a particularly deranged mind with a motive that sane people just could not possibly fathom.

As for who was placing the tiles, the theories run the gamut. It is thought that the tiles in and around Philadelphia are the work of a single person. But were the tiles placed in Chicago by that same person, or is the person in Philadelphia someone who is inspired by a kind of cult of vandals with a desire to spread their message using tiles in asphalt? Again, no one knows for sure.

One theory is that all the tiles were the work of a Philadelphia man who went by the name of James Morasco, who worked in the city as a carpenter. Back in the early 1980s, a man using that name tried to contact a reporter at several Philadelphia-area newspapers to talk about similar rambling ideas as those presented in the tiles. That Morasco, however, would have been in his mid-70s when the first tiles appeared, and he died in 2003. New tiles have shown up in Philadelphia and other cities since then.

A documentary called *Resurrect Dead: The Mystery of Toynbee Tiles* attempted to find the answer as to who was setting up these tiles and why. The movie makes a strong case for the fact that the person involved might be Severino "Sevy" Verna using the pseudonym James Morasco. The film also says that Verna may be placing the tiles using a car with a hole in the floor while he also broadcasts his messages from that same vehicle using shortwave radio transmitters.

Over time, the size and fonts used in the tiles has changed. Before 2007, the tiles were very small, almost not noticeable by pedestrians. Then, after 2007, larger tiles with larger messages and using a different font began appearing and those were the tiles also found in other cities such as Kansas City and Chicago. Now, in Philly, more tiles have been

showing up since 2007. These tiles have been more like the size and using a similar font to the original tiles, which leads many to think that all of the tiles were the work of the same person all along. But if that were the case, was this same person also traveling all over the country to place tiles?

As for the tiles themselves, it depends on what city you are in as to whether or not you can see them and if they are left where they are or removed by the city. The tiles in Philly, for example, tend to still be there and are visible to this day. Chicago, however, has a very strict battle going on against graffiti. City officials have said that they consider the tiles to be vandalism on par with graffiti and have sent men and spent money to remove them from the city streets.

In Chicago, the tiles have shown up downtown, on main streets. One of the most famous appeared right on Michigan Avenue, just across the street from Grant Park. The tiles were red, white, and blue. Many felt that the tile should be left where it was as if it were a piece of art, but the city did send men to remove the tile. Others have popped up from time to time around Chicago, but they have always been removed.

As for how the messages get where they are, one person says that he found a Toynbee tile that had been freshly laid. In this case the message tile was covered in tar paper, camouflaging it by making it look like part of the street. It was placed in a high traffic area so that numerous cars and buses and trucks would run over it. The weight from the trucks, plus the heating of the asphalt, allowed the tile to be pushed into the asphalt. The wear and tear of the vehicles eventually wore away the tar paper to reveal the message.

As for the tiles, there is no organization anywhere that fights to save the tiles. The tiles have gained national attention, including in the local Chicago news, national news, and National Public Radio. Sometimes the tiles just wear away on their own and sometimes they are dug up when the streets are re-paved. They have also been paved over during the normal course of street maintenance.

Still, the tiles keep appearing. They appear in Chicago, from time to time, but the highest concentration continues to be in Philadelphia. There are plenty of theories, but few answers.

Is it the work of one person who does a lot of traveling? Or has one person inspired many copycats from around the world? And if so, do the copycats really understand what the message is? Does the person who started it even fully understand what the message is? Or, is it the rambling of an insane mind?

No one seems to know and it remains a Chicago mystery as well as a global mystery.

Conclusion
Mysteries Upon Mysteries

Of course, Chicago is not unique among world cities to have mysteries that just seem to have no explanation. Any city having had the history of this one has just about as many, if not more. However, like most cities, there is a hidden side to Chicago that most of the residents do not see. There is always, just a short breath away from what most people consider "reality," a whole different world of mystery and strangeness. In this world, people can vanish as if they had never been. In this world, UFOs can visit airports and ghosts can haunt old cemeteries. In this world, there are serial killers who masquerade as clowns and fires that destroy homes and lives. In this world, strange broadcasts are the norms and bizarre conspiracy theories are communicated using tiles pressed into streets.

By no means is this a complete list of Chicago's mysteries. Even as this book is being written, people are vanishing and murders are going unsolved. Right now, a strange event that defies explanation might be occurring somewhere in this city. Perhaps the next big mystery that will out-do and out-live every one of the mysteries presented in this book is unfolding, baffling investigators and turning lives upside down.

At the same time, any one of these mysteries could be solved at any minute. A body might be found and bring an end to the nightmare that has tortured the Spira family, for example, or a confession could be made. There has been talk of investigators, once again, digging up the lawn where John Wayne Gacy was a maintenance man to look for human remains. A truly logical explanation for the UFO at O'Hare could present itself. The man wearing the Max Headroom mask could come forward or end up caught by the FBI. The man behind the Toynbee Tiles could also be found. In each case, none of these mysteries is beyond the realm of discovery and resolution. Even the mysteries that are centuries old could be waiting for someone with fresh eyes and an inquisitive mind to look at the evidence and come to a new conclusion.

Perhaps that person is you, Dear Reader. Perhaps someone you know. Or, perhaps, you have a mystery of your own. Because, in the end, that's the one unifying thing about all of these mysteries. They all involve average people doing average things when they happen. It's only when they are looked at in hindsight that they become mysteries.

Bibliography

2006 O'Hare International Airport UFO Sighting. Wikipedia, http://en.wikipedia.org/wiki/2006_O'Hare_International_Airport_UFO_sighting

American Airlines Flight 191, Wikipedia. http://en.wikipedia.org/wiki/American_Airlines_Flight_191

Avila, Jim. "Peterson's Missing Blue Containers," *ABC7 News*, December 13, 2007. http://abcnews.go.com/TheLaw/story?id=3993648#.TwN8me5dkuw

Bachelor's Grove Cemetery. Wikipedia, http://en.wikipedia.org/wiki/Bachelor's_Grove_Cemetery

Bachelor's Grove Cemetery (website and blog). http://bachelorsgrovecemetery.blogspot.com/

"Bachelor's Grove & Paranormal Activity." Bachelor's Grove Cemetery & Settlement Recreational Center, http://www.bachelorsgrove.net/bachelors-grove-paranormal-activity.htm

"Bachelor's Grove Cemetery." Haunted Hamilton, http://www.hauntedhamilton.com/gotw_bachelorsgrove.html

Bachelor's Grove Website. http://www.bachelors-grove.com/

Bales, Richard F. "Did the Cow Do It? A New Look at the Cause of the Great Chicago Fire," TheChicagoFire.com. http://www.thechicagofire.com/

Bell, Rachael. "The Tylenol Terrorist," *TruTV*. http://www.trutv.com/library/crime/terrorists_spies/terrorists/tylenol_murders/index.htm

Bellows, Alan. "Remember, Remember the 22nd of November." Damn Interesting. http://www.damninteresting.com/remember-remember-the-22nd-of-november/

Bergmann, Joy. "A Bitter Pill." *Chicago Reader*. http://www.chicagoreader.com/chicago/tylenol-killings-a-bitter-pill/Content?oid=903786

Bielski, Ursula. "Marija: The Half-life of Resurrection Mary," Ghostvillage.com, March 23, 2007. http://www.ghostvillage.com/resources/2007/features_03232007.shtml

Booth, Billy. "2006-O'Hare Airport UFO Sighting, About.com. http://ufos.about.com/od/bestufocasefiles/p/ohareairport.htm

Brach, Helen. Wikipedia. http://en.wikipedia.org/wiki/Helen_Brach

Branch, John. "Police Investigate new Stacy Peterson lead." CNN.com, June 5, 2010. http://articles.cnn.com/2010-06-05/justice/drew.peterson.search_1_drew-peterson-kathleen-saviBro-stacy-peterson?_s=PM:CRIME

"Bruhl, Blough & Miller Indiana Dunes Park: 1966 Missing Illinois Trio Indiana." InvisionFree, March 26, 2006. http://s10.invisionfree.com/usedtobedoe/ar/t896.htm

Carlson, Prescott. "Did a Serial Killer Group Hit Chicago?" *The Chicagoist*. http://chicagoist.com/2008/04/26/did_a_serial_ki.php

Carlyle, Erin. "Dallas Drake puts hit on smiley-face killer theory." *City Pages*, July 14, 2010. http://blogs.citypages.com/blotter/2010/07/smiley-face_kil_1.php

"Chicago's Missing Mother: the Case of Lisa Stebbic." *The Crime Times*, August 31, 2010. http://thecrimetimes.wordpress.com/2010/08/31/chicagos-missing-mother-the-case-of-lisa-stebic/

Chicago Tylenol Murders, Wikipedia. http://en.wikipedia.org/wiki/Chicago_Tylenol_murders

DeBartolo, Anthony. "Who Caused The Great Chicago Fire? A Possible Deathbed Confession." HydeParkMedia. http://www.hydeparkmedia.com/cohn.html

"Fascinating Cold Case: Elsie Paroubek, Killed 1911." Websleuths. com, June, 2006. http://websleuths.com/forums/showthread.php?t=70254

Felion, Marc. "The Search for Kevin Clewer's Killer." Feast of Fun, June 16, 2010. http://feastoffun.com/topics/news-rumors/2010/06/16/fernand/

Find Stacy Peterson (website). http://findstacypeterson.net/

"From Hannah." (Account of trip to Rosehill Cemetery), Ghost to Ghost. http://www.ghosttoghost.com/TheGhostofRosehill.htm

Gacy, John Wayne. Wikipedia. http://en.wikipedia.org/wiki/John_Wayne_Gacy

"Ghosts of Flight 191." Encounters with the Unexplained. http://terrifyingtales.blogspot.com/2006/11/ghosts-of-flight-191.html

"Ghosts of Flight 191." Haunted Places and Urban Legends from Illinois. http://www.hauntedusa.com/flight191.htm

"Ghosts of History Live in Rosehille Cemetery." Cemetery Studies. http://www.angelfire.com/ky2/cemetery/rosehill.html

Gress, John. "Five women killed in Chicago-area store shooting." *Reuters*, February 3, 2008. http://www.reuters.com/article/2008/02/03/us-usa-shooting-store-idUSN0244670020080203

Goudie, Chuck. "Question about Valerie Percy murder outlive her father." *The Daily Herald*, September 18, 2011. http://www.dailyherald.com/article/20110918/news/709189818/

Haines, Richard F. "Report of An Unidentified Aerial Phenomenon and its Safety Implications at O'Hare International Airport on November 7, 2006." National Aviation Reporting Center on Anomalous Phenomena. http://www.narcap.org/reports/TR10_Case_18a.pdf

Hilkevitch, Jon. On his Chicago O'Hare UFO Story (VIDEO). http://www.youtube.com/watch?v=3TVF4c90xGA

Hilkevitch, Jon. "In the Sky! A bird? A plane? A...UFO?, *Chicago Tribune*, January 1, 2007, http://web.archive.org/web/20071117073414/http://www.chicagotribune.com/classified/automotive/columnists/chi-0701010141jan01,0,5874175.column?page=1&coll=chi-newsnationworldiraq-hed

Hosey, Joseph. "Missing Man John Spira's Wife Dead For More Than Six Months — Did Cops Have a Clue?," *Shorewood Patch*, May 12, 2011

"Illinois Police Search for Missing Mom; Husband Thinks Someone Picked Her Up for Exercise Class." FoxNews.com, May 10, 2007. http://www.foxnews.com/story/0,2933,270106,00.html

"John Spira." Community United Effort, Center for Missing Persons, November 25, 2009. http://www.ncmissingpersons.org/tag/john-spira/

Kaye, Randi. "Smiley face killers may be stalking college men." CNN, May 21, 2008. http://articles.cnn.com/2008-05-21/justice/smiley.face.killer_1_mysterious-deaths-killers-nypd-officer?_s=PM:CRIME

"Kidnappers Kill Child: Reward Offered for Abductors of Elsie Paroubek, Found in Canal." *New York Times*, May 12, 1911. http://query.nytimes.com/mem/archive-free/pdf?_r=1&res=9C06EFDB1431E233A25751C1A9639C946096D6CF&oref=slogin

Krajicek, David. "Valerie Percy Murder." *TruTv*. http://www.trutv.com/library/crime/notorious_murders/famous/valerie_percy/index.html

Lane Bryant Shooting. Wikipedia. http://en.wikipedia.org/wiki/Lane_Bryant_shooting

"Max Headroom WTTW Pirating Incident - 11/22/87 (Subtitled)." YouTube.com (video). http://www.youtube.com/watch?v=tWdgAMYjYSs

McCoppin, Robert and Glenn Wall. "Newly disclosed account surfaces in 1966 Valerie Percy murder case: Doctor's written report sheds some light, raises some questions." *Chicago Tribune*, June 14, 2011. http://articles.chicagotribune.com/2011-06-14/news/ct-met-percy-murder-20110614_1_nydia-hohf-first-homicide-murder

Milano, Susan Murphy. "John Spira a Victim of Intimate Partner Homicide?" Monday, April 25, 2011. http://murphymilanojournal.blogspot.com/2011/04/john-spira-victim-of-intimate-partner.html

"Missing Man's Biz Partner Told Stories of Million-Dollar Debt, 'Mysterious Life.'" October 25, 2011. http://www.johnspira.com/b3/2011/10/news-article-about-john-spira-case/

"Missing Man John Spira's Wife Dead For More Than Six Months — Did Cops Have a Clue?" http://shorewood-il.patch.com/articles/missing-man-john-spiras-wife-dead-for-more-than-six-months-did-cops-have-a-clue

Montaldo, Charles. "Clues Sought in Disappearance of Stacy Peterson," About.com, November 4, 2007. http://crime.about.com/b/2007/11/05/clues-sought-in-disappearance-of-stacy-peterson.htm

Murder of the Grimes Sisters. Wikipedia. http://en.wikipedia.org/wiki/Murder_of_the_Grimes_sisters

"Murders that Rocked Gay Community Unsolved After 7 Years." CBS 2 Chicago, March 30, 2011. http://chicago.cbslocal.com/2011/03/30/murders-that-rocked-gay-community-unsolved-after-7-years/

Murray, David. "Unanswered Cries: Drew Peterson Ex-Wife Kathleen Savio's Death." Chicago Magazine, May 2008. http://www.chicagomag.com/Chicago-Magazine/May-2008/Unanswered-Cries/

O'Brien, John. "The St. Valentine's Day Massacre: With one ruthless stroke, Al Capone assumes undisputed leadership of Chicago crime." Chicago Tribune, February 14, 1929. http://www.chicagotribune.com/news/politics/chi-chicagodays-valentinesmassacre-story,0,1233196.story

Oh Henry Ballroom. Wikipedia, http://en.wikipedia.org/wiki/Oh_Henry_Ballroom

O'Hare UFO Leaked News Footage (VIDEO). http://video.google.ca/videoplay?docid=5488895546832717747

Paroubek, Elsie. Wikipedia. http://en.wikipedia.org/wiki/Elsie_Paroubek

Penot, Jessica "The Ghosts of Flight 191,," Ghost Stories and Haunted Places. http://ghoststoriesandhauntedplaces.blogspot.com/2010/04/ghosts-of-flight-191.html

Percy, Charles H. Wikipedia. http://en.wikipedia.org/wiki/Charles_H._Percy

Peterson, Drew. Wikipedia. http://en.wikipedia.org/wiki/Drew_Peterson#Disappearance_of_Stacy_Peterson

Ponce, Dan. "Peterson says he loves, misses fourth wife," ABC News, November 19, 2007. http://abclocal.go.com/wls/story?section=news/local&id=5769607

Potash, Larry. "More Gacy Victims? Police fail to dig in all locations during follow up investigation." WGN TV, March 17, 2011. http://www.wgntv.com/entertainment/viral/wgntv-the-unsolved-murders-of-john-wayne-gacy-mar17,0,2784778.story

Proulx, Mary-Jo. "Kevin Clewer Case Remembered." Windy City Media Group. March 30, 2005. http://www.windycitymediagroup.com/gay/lesbian/news/ARTICLE.php?AID=7784

McQuaid, Russ. "New theories surface on decades-old Indiana Dunes cold case." WXIN, November 5, 2010. http://www.fox59.com/news/wxin-new-theories-surface-on-decade-110510,0,2189234.story

"Resurrection Cemetery." True Illinois Haunts, Haunted Places. http://trueillinoishaunts.com/haunted-places/cemeteries/resurrection-cemetery/

"Resurrection Mary." Unsolved Mysteries (VIDEO). http://www.youtube.com/watch?v=oJReMt4sskA

Resurrection Mary. Wikipedia. http://en.wikipedia.org/wiki/Resurrection_Mary

"Rosehill Cemetery." Ghost Haunters. http://www.ghosthaunters.com/index.php?pr=Rosehill_Cemetery

"Rosehill Cemetery." Haunted Places and Urban Legends from Illinois. http://www.hauntedusa.org/rosehill.htm

"Rosehill Cemetery Investigation." The Ghost Research Society. http://www.ghostresearch.org/Investigations/rosehill.html

Rosehill Cemetery. Wikipedia. http://en.wikipedia.org/wiki/Rosehill_Cemetery

Saint Valentine's Day Massacre, Wikipedia. http://en.wikipedia.org/wiki/Saint_Valentine's_Day_massacre

"Saint Valentine's Day Massacre with Pictures—1929—Al Capone True Crime Story: A True Crime Story of Guns and Gangsters." MysterNet.com. http://www.mysternet.com/vdaymassacre/

Searching for John Spira, the John Spira website. http://www.johnspira.com/

SFKillers.com (website) http://sfkillers.com/

Selzer, Adam. "Mary Bregovy: Resurrection Mary?", Chicago Unbelievable, April 7, 2008. http://www.chicagounbelievable.com/2008/04/mary-bregovy-resurrection-mary.htmlKruse, Karen.

Smiley Face Murder Theory. Wikipedia. http://en.wikipedia.org/wiki/Smiley_face_murder_theory

"Smiley Face Patterns." Smiley Face Murder Investigations. http://surfdete.ipower.com/patterns.html

Springer, John. "Police investigating missing woman's husband Police chief of Plainfield, Ill., tells TODAY that 'foul play' is suspected." MSNBC.com, July 13, 2007. http://today.msnbc.msn.com/id/19743438

"Stacy Ann Peterson Missing Sunday." October 28, 2007—Bolingbrook, Illinois, Candy Rose. http://www.acandyrose.com/stacy_peterson_recap.htm

"Stacy Peterson's Family Releases Audio Tape." WBKO, December 7, 2007. http://www.wbko.com/news/headlines/12257046.html#

"Stacy Peterson's Sister Talks About 4th Anniversary Of Her Disappearance." CBS Chicago, October 25, 2011. http://chicago.cbslocal.com/2011/10/25/stacy-petersons-sister-talks-about-4th-anniversary-of-her-disappearance/

Stebbic, Lisa. Wikipedia, http://en.wikipedia.org/wiki/Lisa_Stebic

Tarma, Michael. "Police describe shooting suspect." NWI.com, February 5, 2008. http://www.nwitimes.com/news/local/police-describe-shooting-suspect/article_bf0078bd-3a2b-5

"Help Solve Kevin Clewer's Murder," 4chicagokev.com. http://www.4chicagokev.com/

Taylor, Troy. "Rosehill Cemetery." Weird and Haunted Chicago. http://www.prairieghosts.com/rosehill.html

Taylor, Troy. "Lingering Spirits of Flight 191." Weird and Haunted Chicago. http://www.prairieghosts.com/flight.html

Thale, Christopher P. "The St. Valentine's Day Massacre," Encyclopedia of Chicago. http://encyclopedia.chicagohistory.org/pages/1191.html

The Great Chicago Fire. Wikipedia. http://en.wikipedia.org/wiki/Great_Chicago_Fire

"The Grimes Sisters Murders and the Ghost Car of German Church Road." Haunt Detective. http://www.hauntdetective.com/index.php?option=com_content&view=article&id=66:grimes-girls&catid=36:southside&Itemid=63

"The Haymarket Affair Digital Collection." Chicago Historical Society. http://www.chicagohs.org/hadc/

"The Haymarket Affair." Homicide in Chicago 1870-1930. http://homicide.northwestern.edu/context/movements/haymarket/

The Haymarket Affair. Wikipedia. http://en.wikipedia.org/wiki/Haymarket_affair

The Max Headroom Broadcast Signal Intrusion. Wikipedia. http://en.wikipedia.org/wiki/Max_Headroom_broadcast_signal_intrusion

The Tinley Park Lane Bryant Murders. "The Tinley Park Shootings." (Collection of articles.) The Southtown Star. http://southtownstar.suntimes.com/news/tpshooting/index.html

"The Tylenol Murders," The History Channel. http://www.history.com/this-day-in-history/the-tylenol-murders

"The Unsolved Crime of the Grimes Sisters," Unsolved-Mysteries.com, July 30, 2007. http://www.unsolved-mysteries.com/crime_mysteries/unsolved_crime_of_the_grimes_sisters.html

"The Unsolved Murders of John Wayne Gacy." Chicago Tribune (video). http://www.chicagotribune.com/videobeta/86e4c8f0-5380-4926-abd2-77dd3f4e22f6/News/The-unsolved-murders-of-John-Wayne-GacyNews/The-unsolved-murders-of-John-Wayne-GacyNews/The-unsolved-murders-of-John-Wayne-GacyNews/The-unsolved-murders-of-John-Wayne-GacyNews/The-unsolved-murders-of-John-Wayne-GacyNews/The-unsolved-murders-of-John-Wayne-GacyNews/The-unsolved-murders-of-John-Wayne-GacyNews/The-unsolved-murders-of-John-Wayne-GacyNews/The-unsolved-murders-of-John-Wayne-GacyNews/The-unsolved-murders-of-John-Wayne-Gacy

"The Unsolved Murder of Kevin Clewer." Unsolved Murder.com. http://www.unsolvedmurder.com/

"Toynbee Tiles—Chicago CBS2 News." YouTube.com (video). http://www.youtube.com/watch?v=Zi0kJlKhVfU

Toynbee Tiles. Wikipedia. http://en.wikipedia.org/wiki/Toynbee_tiles

"UFO At O'Hare? Officials Say Weird Weather." CBS News, February 11, 2009, http://www.cbsnews.com/stories/2007/01/02/tech/main2323918.shtml

UFO over Chicago Airport (VIDEO). http://www.youtube.com/watch?v=u4ptRHt95Yk&feature=related